Treating
Pornography
Addiction

THE ESSENTIAL TOOLS FOR RECOVERY

BY DR. KEVIN B. SKINNER

K. Skinner, Corp.
199 N. 290 W. ste 150
Lindon, Utah 84042
www.discoverandchange.com
www.treating-pornography-addiction.com

PUBLISHED BY:
K. Skinner, Corp.
199 N. 290 W. ste 150
Lindon, Utah 84042
www.discoverandchange.com
www.treating-pornography-addiction.com

ISBN 0-9772208-0-X

Cover and book design by Stephen Hales Creative

*To my wonderful wife and eight
incredible children. No man could
ask for more joy than you give me.*

Contents

Introduction

As John sat down in front of me, I knew the problem before he began to speak. His internal lights were out. He was spent. He had hit the proverbial bottom and was finally ready to admit that he needed help. As John started to tell his long history with masturbation and pornography, he was shaking. He had been dealing with strong sexual feelings for years, actually four years, before he hit puberty. He was tired of wasting so much time each day looking at pornography. He was tired of missing classes and work because he had been up all night looking at pornography. He simply couldn't deny it any longer—he needed help. He was living a lie; he had been living it for fifteen years. Nobody knew of the inner turmoil he was feeling. His parents were great people, but he didn't dare tell them that he was fantasizing, masturbating, and viewing pornography every day. He didn't dare tell them that he was looking at pornography for hours a day. His girlfriend wouldn't understand if he told her that he was looking at pornography every day while they were dating. He couldn't talk with his roommates because they had the same problems. He didn't know where to turn. He couldn't tell his parents, he didn't dare tell his girlfriend, and he was afraid to talk with his religious leaders.

John is one of the many men who have come to therapy seeking a reprieve from an addiction to pornography. Sadly, our society has created an environment where sex is pushed upon us from every angle. It is on TV, the Internet, billboards, in magazines—virtually everywhere we look, sexual images are thrust upon us. While we are inundated with pornographic images, we don't have an outlet to discuss what these images are doing to our minds. One young man put it this way.

> Growing up, my family didn't talk about sex. The only thing I knew about girls was that I had to show them respect. My dad reinforced this by yelling at me if I said or did anything disrespectful to my mom. When I got to college and my roommates

were talking about masturbating in the shower and what they had done with their girlfriends the previous night, I was shocked. I had no clue such a world existed. My curiosity led me to start acting out too, and it didn't take long before I was just one of the boys. I talked about the same things and I was soon doing the same things with the girls I was dating. The problem came for me when I was exposed to pornography. From the first time I saw it, I got such a high off it that I was instantly addicted. I began viewing it every chance I could. Obviously, I couldn't tell my roommates that I had a problem; they would have laughed me out of apartment. I wouldn't tell my parents in a million years. Soon I became depressed and hopeless. I had violated my own belief and value system and didn't have anyone to talk to about my feelings.

When clients begin to tell their stories for the first time it is like they are unleashing years of pent up venom. They realize they don't have to continue to maintain their secret lifestyle. For the first time in their lives they are able to share their hidden secret. This is the beginning of the healing process. When the secret is finally disclosed and they don't feel judged or looked down upon, they realize that they have been hurting themselves for months and often years.

In the fall of 2001, a well-respected religious leader approached me and asked if I would be willing to work with some of the young men he was trying to help overcome pornography addiction. He said it was a growing problem and that he needed a professional therapist upon whom he could rely. Previous to discussing this possibility with him, I too had begun to see an increase in pornography related referrals. In fact, at one point the agency where I was working had eleven referrals to review during our staff meeting. Seven of the referrals were individuals struggling to overcome pornography addiction.

Since that time, much of the work I have done is with individuals and couples who have been deeply impacted by pornography and its insidious effects. Some have lost their spouse. Others have had to pull out of college because they couldn't focus on their schooling. Still others have been so depressed that they felt hopeless. Their lives are out of control and they don't know what to do to stop their own behavior.

What I want to say to those who feel hopeless and helpless is that there is hope. The journey may be long and intimidating but answers are available. The helpless and powerless feeling you are experiencing can be replaced by hope and joy. This workbook is an introduction to help the down trodden and weary break the cycle of pornography addiction.

I am not claiming that this book will stop the temptations or eliminate your desires to view pornography; that comes through consistent and persistent use of the tools that will be described in this book. This book will, however, provide the right tools to fight the battle. When these tools are incorporated into day-to-day living, the result is more confidence and hope that change is possible. By actively working on the principles discussed in this book, I know that the battle can be won. I have witnessed hope return to the lives of individuals who have felt trapped. I have seen confidence return where it had been lost. It is possible. My hope is that these principles will help restore energy and vitality into the lives of those who have had pornography drain the energy of life from their very souls.

May God bless you in your journey,

—Dr. Kevin B. Skinner, LMFT

Chapter 1:
The Creation of a Pornography Addiction

I have heard many stories as a therapist. Sometimes I want to shake my head in disbelief. It is hard to fathom the awful things some people have to face. Such was the case with Eric. He grew up in a small rural town with his mom and stepdad. At age four he remembers hearing the constant arguing and fighting. His stepdad had pornographic magazines strewn all over the house and his mom was forever trying to prevent him from looking at them. However, she couldn't keep up; they were everywhere. As the arguments and fighting increased at home, Eric found satisfaction in viewing these pornographic magazines. They brought him comfort and excitement when he was feeling alone or sad. They became his safe haven.

When arguing with her husband (and because she didn't want her son to get hit or be verbally abused), Eric's mom would give him a pornographic magazine just to keep him away from the fighting. Unwittingly, his mother reinforced his feeling of finding comfort and safety in the magazines. Soon thereafter, Eric was looking at magazines every time he felt sad or alone. During Eric's teen years he often turned to pornography and masturbation. As he matured into adulthood, pornography wasn't enough; his behavior then turned into one-night sexual experiences and unhealthy relationships.

This story illustrates what many individuals with pornography addiction are dealing with. Some of the key elements in the development of addictions are present in Eric's case. These elements include: starting at a young age, controlling or uninvolved parents, loneliness and isolation, seeing a model of unhealthy relationships, a negative social system, and early childhood sexual abuse.

YOUNG AGE

Most addicts get started at a young age. In a majority of my cases, the earlier the exposure to pornography, the deeper the client's level of addiction. In most cases I see involvement with pornography starting between ages ten to fourteen. Children get exposed to pornography at a friend's house, an older brother's magazine stash, a parent's DVD, R-rated movies, the Sears catalogue, advertisements, and, most recently, online via pornographic emails, pop-up windows, and in some cases by accident.

In today's society each of us is constantly being exposed to some form of sexual image or sexual innuendo. Our children are no different. They are being forced to deal with sexual issues long before they should be. An eight year old should not be exposed to a parent's X-rated videos. Children should not be exposed to unwanted sexual images over the Internet, but they are. One researcher found that one in four children who use the Internet is exposed to unwanted sexual material.[1] The effect of this exposure was well described in Alexander Pope's essay on man:

> *Vice is a monster of so frightful mien*
> *As to be hated needs but to be seen*
> *Yet seen too oft, familiar with her face,*
> *We first endure, then pity, then embrace.*

Sadly, our society has followed this pattern. The sexual exposure we face is unparalleled in the history of mankind. With television, the Internet, magazines, billboards, movies, and DVDs, our society has been desensitized. As a glaring statement on our society, author Andy Butcher wrote, "For the twenty-year-old kid, porn stars have kind of replaced what models used to represent."[2]

The result of this desensitization process is that children and teenagers are faced with sexual decisions before they fully understand the consequences of their own sexual behaviors. A teenager caught up in Internet pornography doesn't understand that his curiosity can lead to an addiction. One young man said, "At first it was curiosity, then it turned into something

I would do before I masturbated. Now it is something I question whether I will ever be able to stop."

Unfortunately, many of these children and teens do not have someone to give them a reality check. Even in cases in which the family is intact, teenagers and adults do not want to admit that there is a problem. It has been taboo to talk about sexual things, especially pornography. Consequently, most children and adults keep their secret inside and develop this addiction. For years they bottle it up, fearing that if someone ever finds out they will be punished, cast-out, rejected, made fun of, or otherwise castigated.

While exact statistics don't exist on how many children exposed to pornography actually become addicted to it, it is fair to say that too many are dealing with out-of-control feelings and are unable to quit. Many of the high school and college students I meet say they want to stop, but they relapse far too often for their own comfort.

CONTROLLING OR DISENGAGED PARENTS

A majority of individuals who struggle with addictions live in homes where their parents are very strict, rigid, and controlling, or they are disinterested or disengaged in their child's life. In Eric's case for example, his mother was trying her level best to raise her son, but she was dealing with her own relationship issues. In trying to protect her son from witnessing the physical violence and yelling, she became disengaged, not intentionally, but out of necessity for her own survival.

In other instances, parents who are strict and controlling can also contribute to an addiction. This comes in the form of guilt loading, also referred to as shaming a child. Children who are often shamed turn to behaviors that are comforting. They are looking for something to soothe the emotional rejection they feel when they have been shamed. One client said it this way, "I could never please my mother. No matter what I did, it was never good enough. She would criticize almost everything I did. Eventually I learned that I had to lie to my mom to avoid being shamed. Eventually I didn't even recognize when I was lying or telling the truth."

Research is clear that children who grow up in controlling and manipulative homes often develop unhealthy coping mechanisms. Consequently, if a child is exposed to pornography and sexual behaviors during this time of learning to cope with controlling parents, it is predictable that he will turn to these things when in emotional pain.

LONELINESS AND ISOLATION

In situations in which viewing pornography escalates into an addiction, loneliness and isolation are often key contributors to the problem. Eric reported he would spend many hours alone. In one instance he spent several days all by himself. He felt abandoned. He related that during long periods of isolation he found comfort in viewing pornography. Many of my clients cite loneliness as an important contributing factor when they view pornography. This is especially true for individuals who are single and have no current hope in finding a relationship. They often say, "Why try? No one would ever want me anyway."

Others are shy or experience social anxiety when they think about relationships. They feel intimidated by social settings and often turn to pornography as a coping mechanism when they are overwhelmed by their social inadequacies. In such situations their feelings of loneliness stem from their fears of being rejected or made fun of. Professionals call this social anxiety. Fortunately, shyness and social anxiety can be overcome by learning new social skills, but seldom does this happen without the addiction to pornography being resolved first.

Clearly, a critical step to recovery, regardless of what the addiction is, is to learn how to interact with others in social settings. Isolation and loneliness are devastating feelings for pornography addicts trying to recover. Without social support their isolation leads them to feel like no one cares about them. They begin to intentionally isolate themselves out of frustration and even retaliation for the social rejection that they feel. They become victims via the feelings generated in their own minds.

Ironically, the pornography that many are turning to creates an even deeper feeling of isolation. These vicarious relationships create a new kind of loneliness—the loneliness of people whose relationships are with images and illusions instead of persons.

There are some instances where children self-create their isolation. They have parents who are involved in their lives but they still develop an addiction to pornography. In these situations the child is creating a double image or personality. He creates one persona with his parents and in society, and another one when he is alone. In these situations my experience has been that these children were exposed at an early age to pornography (at a friend's house, when they were at home alone with nothing to do but play on the computer, etc.) and developed their own little secret behavior.

This was the case with Matt. He grew up with parents who were very supportive. They had high standards and he really felt close to his dad. He was a good student and participated in sports and other social activities. His parents were proud of him and everyone told him what a good kid he was. However, Matt spent a lot of time alone after school with both of his parents working. At age fourteen he found Internet pornography. What started as initial curiosity turned into a real problem, and by age sixteen he was looking at pornography almost daily. He felt guilty, and finally at age seventeen he confided in his religious leader. He explained to this leader that he had a problem with pornography and he didn't know how to overcome it. His leader encouraged him to stop and told him that everything would be okay if he would read the scriptures and pray daily.

Over the next few months and years he tried to stop but he couldn't do it by himself. By the time he sought professional help he was in his midtwenties. He had formed many beliefs about himself. He believed he was flawed in some way and he felt alone and guilty. His guilt became so overwhelming that he was depressed to the point that he wasn't sure of himself. He was convinced that he would never be able to quit looking at pornography.

He didn't think his parents would accept him. He had this secret and he believed nobody would ever understand him.

Only when he opened up and honestly started talking with others did he realize he wasn't alone. His mind had trapped itself in a corner to the point that he thought he was alone on a deserted island. When Matt learned he had a support team around him, he felt empowered and hopeful. As Matt's story vividly illustrates, loneliness and isolation are devastating for individuals struggling to overcome a pornography addiction.

MODEL OF UNHEALTHY RELATIONSHIPS

Individuals with pornography addiction often develop unhealthy ideas about relationships. Many pornography addicts grow up in homes where there is not an example of how people should treat each other. In Eric's case, he saw his mom surviving a relationship. He saw many men (potential father figures) enter and leave his life. He never had a dad figure to teach him. The only lessons he learned from his stepdad were that pornography and sex are very important. As Eric matured he had no model of how to treat women. He came to therapy because his fiancé was concerned about his pornography and masturbation problem. He had reluctantly told her and she refused to marry him unless he got professional help. Only after exploring his history did Eric admit all of his struggles with pornography, masturbation, and pushing women beyond their comfort zone. He acknowledged he had no idea how a man should treat a woman. He indicated that he saw women as objects to "score" with.

Others see and experience sexual advances and innuendos as common behavior in their homes. There are no boundaries growing up. They are sexualized at an early age. They are exposed to pornography, R-rated and X-rated videos, and other sexual behaviors at such an early age, and they do not comprehend the need to establish sexual boundaries in relationships. When children are sexualized at an early age they often mistake sex for love in relationships. This perception can lead to one unhealthy relationship after another.

Pornography can also change a person's view of the purpose and function of a relationship. If a relationship is solely looked upon as a sexual experience it may initially be exciting, but it is built upon a weak foundation that will eventually crumble. Sexual intimacy in relationships is just one element of what creates a healthy long-term bond, and when the other areas of intimacy are not developed, problems will arise.

Many single and married men are concerned about being attracted to the women in their lives because their wives or girlfriends don't have the same physique as the women in the pornography they view. Pornographic movies and images are so unrealistic that men who see these images can only be let down by reality. Further, some men worry their expectations about the sexual relationship are significantly different from their spouse's, and probably unrealistic. The truth is, pornography can warp a person's view of what a healthy husband and wife sexual relationship can be. When a person's perspective of how men and women should treat each other becomes distorted in this way, what should be a deeply intimate experience is devalued into merely a simple physical act.

Moreover, pornography hurts relationships because it is often done in secret. Secrets, especially related to sex and pornography, are destructive to relationships because they hurt the trust and feelings of loyalty necessary for healthy relationships to exist. Almost all pornography addicts feel the need to keep their pornography from their spouse or others. In maintaining this secret, the addict limits how close he lets others get to him, because in living a lie it is hard to create real intimacy. Many people try to fake closeness, but in living a lie or creating a double identity it is virtually impossible to create healthy relationships.

Heavy involvement in pornography will never lead to a healthy relationship. As a professional, I have never seen a person deeply involved in pornography who hasn't either had a relationship problem or who fears getting involved in relationships because he is scared no one would want him because of his addiction to pornography.

NEGATIVE SOCIAL SYSTEM

Our society does not prevent children or adults from being exposed to pornography. In the past, pornography was taboo. Someone wanting to purchase pornographic material would have to find a back alley shop hidden away from mainstream traffic. Today, billboard advertisements give directions to their stores in many cities across the country. These same billboards have images of women on them that would have been outright rejected in the past.

Due to the financial power of those who make pornography, many turn their cheek to those who are pushing the boundaries. For example, 75 percent of prime time television in the 1999–2000 season included sexual content.[3] Family Safe Media reported that 2.5 billion pornographic emails are sent out each day, which translates into the average email account receiving 3.1 pornography emails each day,[4] while the pornography industry (sex sites) is growing at a tremendous rate. In the United States alone, sex sites are generating at least 2.5 billion dollars each year.[5] While the Internet sex sites are generating an inordinate amount of money, pornographic adult video and DVD rentals have skyrocketed with 800 million rentals each year, amassing over 20 billion dollars in revenue.[6] The consequence of this type of exposure will be felt for decades to come. We have no idea of the deep and lasting impact this will have on our society.

While society ignores this problem, pornography and sex addiction rates are reaching new heights every year. We will wake up in a few years and have an epidemic of incredible proportions with no way of turning back. Our social system has allowed greed and money to destroy the lives of men, women, and their children. Families are being destroyed, while those who produce such media are reaping the financial benefits.

Meanwhile, peer pressure and a strong cultural influence in various settings (i.e., work, school, activities) has increased. Listening to the radio a while ago, I heard a local sports radio station promoting its calendar, which had its sex models on it. Commercials today contain sexual images or content because they sell. It doesn't matter where we are today, society is pushing sex because it generates money. Sex sells.

A wise man once said, "Constant dripping weareth away the strongest stone." The drip has turned into a steady stream and it is tearing at the very fibers of our society. Because pornography and sex have such a forceful pull on us, if left unchecked our society will erode before our very eyes. We will have millions of people who have sexual addictions, pornography being just one of them.

EARLY SEXUAL EXPERIENCES

In some cases pornography is not the starting point. Sometimes a child has early sexual experiences that start with simple experimentation and turn into more acting out. Early childhood sexual experiences are common. Many children report sexual play with other children. In fact, one in four girls and one in six boys report sexual abuse or play as a child. These early sexual experiences prime children for the time they are exposed to pornography.

Early sexual experiences (including exposure to pornography) are premature for a child's mind. A child's mind cannot make sense of what a sexual experience means. He doesn't understand the feelings that accompany curiosity and embarrassment. Children may have been taught that sexual things were not appropriate, but that doesn't match the enjoyable feelings they may have felt with early sexual experiences. Because early sexual experiences are so profound to the child's mind he can become fixated on sexual thoughts and feelings. Some researchers suggest that strong negative emotional experiences stunt a person's emotional development and maturity. When emotional development slows and the mind gets stuck on sexual feelings, a serious sexual addiction is the likely outcome.

We have learned that our genes can be turned up and down. For example, parents of a child who is genetically predisposed to be shy can actually help alter their child's make up by creating experiences for their child to get out of his or her comfort zone. If this is the case with shyness, is it possible that we can do the same with a child who is exposed to early sexual experiences? Can we turn a generation of children onto sex by giving them early sexual stimulation with pornography or sexual abuse? I believe so. We can alter a person's sexuality by creating a sexual or non-sexual environment for him. Therefore, protecting ourselves and our children from unnecessary exposure is a big step to preventing a sexual addiction.

When exposed to pornography, children who have had early childhood sexual experiences often have their minds brought back to the sexual sensations they felt at an earlier age. These feelings can be exciting and confusing. The exciting feeling is normal because we are sexual beings and sexual experiences generate chemicals that are released into our bodies. The excitement comes from the curiosity of exploring something that reminds them of an earlier feeling. It can also bring back images or feelings that they may have fantasized about because they remember the highly stimulating experience from earlier in their life. No longer do they have to fantasize; they can visually experience images that remind them of those feelings.

Confusion comes from the excited feeling. Children don't want to feel this excitement, and they do not understand the high they feel. Confusion can also come from the fear of being caught or from the bad feeling that came with the early sexual experience. These feelings often catch people off guard because many feel like they have dealt with those earlier issues. In many instances, strong sexual feelings are unwanted and fear provoking, but without the right outlet to discuss these experiences, children, adolescents, and even adults struggle to make sense of their own sexuality.

Each of the elements listed above has a significant impact on the development of an addiction. While healing does not occur by knowing exactly how and why the addiction developed, it does come when the addict learns to put these experiences into perspective by acknowledging how these experiences have had an impact. Then, with this knowledge he will know how to do things differently in the future.

The questions below are designed to help a person identify how each of the areas listed above have contributed to the addictive behavior.

Exercise 1: *As you think about your first exposure to pornography, think about your age at that time. Can you recall your feelings? How did early exposure impact your childhood? If you had not seen pornography at such a young age, how do you think your life would have been different up to this point?*

Exercise 2: *When you consider your parents' parenting style, would you consider them involved or uninvolved? Controlling or lenient? Caring or uncaring? Did your parents' style of parenting contribute to your involvement with pornography?*

Exercise 3: *Have feelings of loneliness contributed to your viewing pornography? In other words, have you turned to pornography because you feel lonely? When you look at pornography, what percentage of the time do you look because you are lonely? Do you feel isolated by others, or do you isolate yourself because of your involvement with pornography? If you isolate yourself, what can you do to become more involved so that isolation doesn't lead you into relapse?*

Exercise 4: *Do you feel like you saw a good model of how a relationship should work growing up? Please explain your answer. Is there any link between your viewing pornography and feeling or sensing relationship stress in your home of upbringing?*

Exercise 5: *How would you say the social system (TV, Internet, movies, etc.) has impacted your perception of pornography? How has the media contributed to your viewing pornography? Would you agree or disagree that the availability has contributed to your problem with pornography? If you could change the availability of pornographic material, would that help you, or do you think you would still seek out pornography?*

Exercise 6: *If you experienced some form of early childhood sexual abuse or childhood sexual experiences, do you feel this impacted your* *involvement with pornography? If so, how? Did you feel an increase in your curiosity and desire to experience or see sexual things? Please explain your answer.*

20   *Dr. Kevin B. Skinner, LMFT*

Chapter 2:
Understanding and Assessing the Levels of Pornography Addiction

Do you remember the first time you thought you might have a problem with pornography? Was it early in your exposure to pornography or has it come to your attention more recently? Many people don't realize that they have a problem until there is either a consequence due to their viewing it (i.e., embarrassment of someone catching them, losing a job, etc.) or they try to stop and find it more difficult to stop than they thought it would be.

A common human response when doing something wrong is to minimize the extent of the problem. Therefore, most addicts deceive themselves into thinking their behavior is not as bad as it really is. This lesson was best illustrated to me by one of my clients. She came to my office and declared that her husband was having an affair. She started by discussing her husband's involvement with pornography. She had been trying for years to get him to address the issue. She dragged him to two therapists. Both were satisfied that pornography wasn't the problem when her husband openly admitted that he looked at pornography every few months, but wasn't involved anymore. They didn't ask further questions when he admitted to looking at it. They were satisfied that if he was only looking at it every few months it wasn't a problem.

By the time she came to my office her husband had been lying to her for many years. In addition to his pornography involvement he had been having affairs and was visiting topless bars. Pornography was the only manifestation of his more deeply seeded sexual addiction, but that wasn't explored in therapy; he had clearly minimized the extent of his problem. I have often wondered if the previous therapists had acknowledged his wife's concern and attempted to assess an addiction to pornography or other sexual behaviors if the outcome would have been different. Perhaps he wasn't ready or willing to honestly deal with his behaviors, but had a thorough assessment been done, what would they have learned and how would that have changed their approach to therapy?

The purpose of this chapter is to give the reader the opportunity to do an honest self-evaluation. You will be given a chance to look at your own level of pornography involvement. It has been my experience that a deep and honest response and self-evaluation is where real healing takes place. Dr. David Viscott's statement, "If you lived honestly, your life would heal itself,"[1] is something to live by if you want to begin the recovery process. Since it is a common behavior to minimize negative actions or to discount the impact of misbehaviors and how they affect others, the focus of the following section is to give you the opportunity to gain self-awareness into your involvement with pornography.

KEY AREAS FOR ASSESSING A PORNOGRAPHY ADDICTION

In order to assess pornography addiction we must first define addiction. The word addiction is a term used to describe an uncontrollable compulsion to repeat a behavior regardless of its negative consequences. Pornography addiction is the compulsive attempt(s) to meet legitimate emotional needs through viewing pornography and seeking sexual gratification, generally through masturbation. There are many behaviors that can lead to a pattern of actions that most professionals recognize as addiction. For example, some of the common signs include, but are not limited to, craving for more of the behavior, increased physiological tolerance to exposure, and withdrawal symptoms in the absence of the stimulus. These are three common signs of addiction.

A challenge to assessing pornography addiction arises because most addiction assessment tools have been adapted from the criteria of other addictive behaviors. Many of the tools for assessing sexually related addictions are relatively new. For example, the criteria for assessing a sexual addiction is less than ten years old and is still not part of the diagnostic manual for mental health professionals. After reviewing many of the lists that assess addiction, and after identifying the key areas that make up an addiction, I believe Dr. Patrick Carnes's list is very useful. I have adapted the list below from the criteria he outlined for a sexual addiction.

CRITERIA FOR PORNOGRAPHY ADDICTION

- Recurrent failure to resist impulses to view pornography
- More extensive/longer viewing of pornography than intended
- Ongoing, but unsuccessful, efforts to stop, reduce, or control behavior
- Inordinate amount of time spent obtaining pornography, viewing pornography, and/or being sexual—either through masturbation, or with another person or object, or recovering from sexual experiences
- Feeling preoccupied with fantasy, sexualized thoughts, and/or preparatory activities
- Viewing pornography takes significant time away from obligations: occupational, academic, domestic, or social
- Continuation of behavior despite consequences
- Tolerance—more frequent or intense pornography is needed over time to obtain the desired result
- Deliberately limiting social, occupational, or recreational activities in order to keep time open for finding and viewing pornography
- Distress, restlessness, or irritability if unable to view pornography (withdrawal)
  a. dizziness
  b. body aches
  c. headaches
  d. sleeplessness
  e. restlessness

f. anxiety

g. mood swings

h. depression

The criteria listed above are the most common signs to look for in assessing a pornography addiction. If pornography addiction behaviors parallel sexual addiction, then a minimum of three of the above ten are needed for a pornography addiction to be considered present. Dr. Carnes has found that most sex addicts have five signs, while over 50 percent have seven.[2]

Utilizing these criteria and my personal clinical experience I have developed the "Assessing Pornography Addiction" test. This test evaluates an individual's personal level of involvement in pornography and explores seven separate and unique levels of involvement or addiction to pornography. This test can be found in Appendix B or at **www.discoverandchange.com/apa** the online version of this test offers personalized feedback and graphs based on the answers provided by the respondent. The seven levels of involvement and the criteria used to assess this will be discussed below.

THE ADDICTION CONTINUUM—7 LEVELS OF PORNOGRAPHY ADDICTION

I believe it is much easier to view pornography involvement and addiction on a continuum rather than proclaiming a person addicted or not addicted. Human behavior generally vacillates in and out of addictive behaviors. When identifying an addiction there are some defining characteristics. First, it is a compulsive behavior or it includes a loss of control. Second, negative consequences are associated with having an addiction. Even with these definitions, we seldom find that a person stays static in his involvement with addictive behaviors. It is more common to see a person's commitment and desire to stop viewing pornography wax and wane with time and circumstances.

For example, some individuals will binge for days or weeks at a time and then remain abstinent for months and even years at a time. This begs the question of why this happens. A clear answer comes from understanding what is happening in each individual's life. His involvement generally fluctuates based on stress, family circumstances, emotional well-being, relationship status, and a host of other reasons. With this understanding, it is helpful to view a person's pornography involvement on levels of a continuum.

In each of the seven levels of pornography addiction there are common behaviors that distinguish each level from the others. The most significant differences in the levels can be found in the consequences of the behaviors: the compulsivity, the frequency and intensity of the behavior, and the beliefs an individual forms about self. As you evaluate yourself it is helpful to understand that you will likely change levels on a regular basis. When you are sincerely trying to limit your involvement, your level of involvement will decrease. When your desire for change and feelings of hope dissipate, you will find your involvement increases toward the higher levels. Below is a continuum that illustrates the seven levels. You will also find a short introduction to each level.

Levels:
|——|——|——|——|——|——|
1   2   3   4   5   6   7

LEVEL I

Level one pornography participation is the mildest form of involvement with pornography a person can have. Generally, those at level one have just recently been exposed to pornography or they only look at pornography once or twice a year. Relatively speaking, these individuals have very limited exposure to pornography. They can count the number of times they have seen nudity on one hand. Their thoughts and everyday actions are not focused on pornography. If they view pornography it is a random act or something that happens by accident. While their exposure to pornography may be limited, they still have to watch carefully not to let their initial exposure increase into a more consistent viewing of pornography.

LEVEL 2

Level two pornography involvement does not indicate that a person has an addiction. At this point, viewing pornography is not a compulsive act nor has it created a lot of problems. The desire to view pornography does not dominate day-in and day-out thinking. Generally speaking, those who score at this level have recently had an increase in exposure to pornography and are questioning the growing curiosity they feel inside.

At level two some pornographic magazines or pornographic Internet sites have been viewed. Episodes of involvement are a few times each year, no more than six. Fantasies are very minimal if at all. The challenge at this level is that there is a growing curiosity. The time spent thinking about or viewing pornography is still relatively limited, but the growing interest can escalate quickly. This is especially true if recent behaviors make a person want more and more exposure.

LEVEL 3

Level three pornography involvement is on the borderline between a growing problem and a compulsive behavior—a sign of addiction. Individuals involved at level three are likely looking at pornography about once a month and this has probably been going on for a while. Those who are at this level try to restrain themselves from more exposure, but about once a month it becomes unbearable and they give in. Once they do give in it is likely they will binge for a day or two before attempting to stop again.

There are some individuals at this level who don't consider their involvement to be a problem. They feel like they can manage their behaviors on their own, and in most instances they try to monitor their behavior and limit their exposure. These individuals are at a crossroads, as further involvement is more likely to become compulsive in nature. Generally speaking, individuals at level three have to put extra effort into quitting entirely because they have been exposed to stronger forms of pornography (R-rated videos, nude pictures, sexual movies, etc.).

Fantasizing is also a part of the battle at level three. As their mind tries to avoid thinking about pornography, they still find themselves fantasizing about viewing it. The challenge is that fantasizing at this level makes it more and more difficult to *not* give in to viewing pornography. It is common for individuals at level three to start spending extra time and energy fighting off thoughts of pornography and the desire to view it. They may even start to feel some of the withdrawal symptoms if they don't give in. Consequently, individuals at level three can quickly escalate into higher levels of involvement. Generally speaking, those who score at this level have recently had an increase in exposure to pornography and are starting to think more and more about pornography and sexual things.

LEVEL 4

At level four, involvement with pornography is likely impacting more and more aspects of a person's life. At this level individuals often begin to wonder why they are thinking so much about pornography. Their involvement may even be surprising to themselves. The consequences of their behaviors are likely influencing more than just themselves. It may be impacting their ability to focus on tasks for work, school, family life, or relationships. They are viewing pornography a few times each month and are looking at more hard-core types of pornography. They are likely viewing movies or downloading clips from the Internet.

It is likely that their fantasizing has increased. Often individuals at level four spend time fantasizing about sexual things even if they do not act out their fantasies. They are getting their high off thinking about pornographic images, but they don't feel as bad because they aren't actually looking at pornography. When individuals regularly fantasize they receive a natural high that is often a sign that an escalated behavior such as intense pornography viewing or acting out is about to happen.

It is common for individuals at level four to fight off strong urges and desires to view pornography. Therefore, at this level you will see an increase in withdrawal symptoms (restlessness, irritability, insomnia, etc.). Individuals at level four may be viewing pornography every other week or so, but their desire to give in between episodes is often strong and challenging. Consequently, individuals at level four can quickly escalate into higher levels of involvement by viewing pornography weekly and sometimes more.

Generally speaking, those who score at level four have been fighting pornography for many years. They may have cut back or tried to stop, but find they can only go a couple of weeks without giving in to the desire. There are also individuals who are just beginning to experience escalated behaviors and feel a strong compulsion to view pornography every other week. At this point, most people are more involved in pornography than they want to be. They may feel like they have tried to stop so many times that it is hopeless. Many wonder why it is so hard to stop. The risk for moving into more intense pornography viewing from this level is high. If a person can acknowledge there is a problem at this level, he can often head off more deeply seeded compulsive behaviors.

LEVEL 5

At level five, pornography is impacting regular day-to-day living. At this level, individuals are spending a significant amount of time each week thinking about pornography. There isn't a day that goes by when they don't think about looking at pornography or give in and looking at it. They are viewing pornography three to five times a week. Pornography and sexual behaviors are probably among the top seven things they think about each day. Pornography is influencing their lives in a significant way.

Often at level five we find individuals who are also dealing with some type of loss. Since pornography is such a big part of their life, they have likely found it has impacted other areas of their life (e.g., work, education, relationships, religious involvement). At lower levels they were able to manage their life and their involvement in pornography without a lot of complications. Now, viewing pornography may be limiting their personal growth and development. In some instances it may have even resulted in losing aspects of their life that used to be important to them.

What initially may have been a hobby or something that was done for entertainment is now a big part of this person's life. Generally speaking, individuals at level five have to put extra effort into quitting entirely because they have been exposed to stronger forms of pornography (R-rated movies, X-rated movies, movie clips, streamline videos, etc.).

Individuals at level five often spend a significant amount of time fantasizing about sexual things. Their fantasies usually lead to viewing pornography. It is common for individuals at level five to begin feeling overwhelmed or consumed with their level of pornography involvement. They begin to experience more intense withdrawal symptoms the longer they go without pornography. They are on the brink of giving up their fight with it. This is what transitions them into level six pornography involvement. It is when a person begins to feel helpless and throws caution to the wind that he transitions to level six. At level six there are no barriers. Level six is when pornography consumes all of a person's daily activities; there is no more fight or desire to stop at that level.

Generally speaking, those who score at level five have been fighting pornography for many years. They may have cut back or tried to stop, but find they can only go a few days without giving into the desire. At this point most people are more involved in pornography than they want to be, but they don't know how to stop on their own. This can generate a hopeless feeling that often leads a person back to viewing pornography.

LEVEL 6

At level six, pornography begins to dominate a person's life. There are very few days he doesn't view pornography. He spends a significant amount of time each day thinking about pornography and sexual things. Initially, pornography was for excitement and entertainment, but over time pornography has become more than just entertainment—it has become a compulsive addiction.

At level six, compulsive behaviors and actions are common. Individuals at this level are likely to feel out of control. This is manifest by the amount of time they are spending with pornographic materials. It has filtered its way into other areas of their life (e.g., relationships, work, school, limited fun times, etc.). There isn't a day that goes by that they don't think about looking at pornography or give in and look at it. Many at this level are viewing pornography daily.

There is also a good chance this level of involvement with pornography has created many situations where a person has had to lie to cover up his activities. Those at this level often lie about what they are doing or how they are spending their time. They have likely created their own stash of pornographic videos and magazines. Their computer has a significant amount of downloaded pornographic clips and they are likely spending a lot of money on pornography (e.g., sex sites, videos).

It is also common for individuals at this level to have been caught and they are starting to feel the negative consequences that are often associated with this level of pornography involvement. Even with the potential negative consequences, they are still willing to take risks and give in to compulsive desires.

Individuals in this situation either have a strong desire to stop viewing pornography or they have completely given up because they feel it is hopeless. The desire to quit may be present, but the counter feeling of giving up is so strong that they feel hopeless. This feeling of hopelessness often exacerbates the problem and creates further sadness and depression, which in turn leads to viewing pornography.

Often at level six we find individuals who are also dealing with some type of loss. They are likely to have lost something in their life due to their involvement with pornography. Some people lose a job, others their spouse, others lose their desire for other passions. Still others lose their belief in God. Such is the power of pornography on the human mind at this level of involvement.

LEVEL 7

At level seven, viewing pornography and sexually acting out are almost daily occurrences. There is a deep seeded compulsive feeling to act out. These feelings impact a person's ability to focus, except on pornography and sex. There is a feeling of powerlessness and hopelessness at this level. There are very few days when pornography is not viewed at this level.

Each day is generally filled with finding and viewing pornography. The images seen are often hardcore and may be filled with violence, rape, incest, bestiality, and other extremely hardcore material. The reason for this escalation is that previous images are no longer stimulating. Most individuals at level seven are engaged in acting out their sexual fantasies. Those who try to limit or curtail how much they view pornography at this level have found that it is virtually impossible to do so on their own. In fact, many at this level have lost their resolve to quit and only try because of the consequences if they don't. Many have been court ordered to seek help.

Individuals at this level feel out of control. They spend hours each day looking for and finding pornography or sex. Pornography has definitely hindered the following areas of this person's life: relationships, work, school, fun and enjoyment, spirituality, and finances.

Lying is a frequent behavior of individuals at level seven. There are many situations each day in which lying has to take place in order to cover up the time spent on pornography and acting out. If caught at this level, there is a good chance this person will minimize his level of involvement because of the potential consequences. The negative consequences at this level are often far reaching and intimidating for the addicted person to deal with.

At level seven the individual's mind time (meaning the things he thinks about when he is alone, at work, or even talking with others) is dominated by thoughts of pornography and sex. In fact, most people at level seven find that if they aren't acting out, they are fantasizing about what they want to do. Once a person starts acting out his fantasies and what he is seeing in pornographic films, he is in a dangerous place because of the risky behaviors in which he is engaged.

Often the devastating effects of level seven involvement are not seen for many months and sometimes years. Families are destroyed; jobs are lost. In almost every case I have seen, level seven pornography involvement includes some form of loss. Such is the addictive power of pornography.

THE CONTINUUM AND SELF-AWARENESS

In my experience in treating pornography addiction it has been a great benefit to see and understand that clients are at different levels of involvement. Understanding this makes it easier to understand their needs and assist them with the best treatment protocol. Many of my clients have sought help when they were compulsively acting out (levels 5–7). While in this level of involvement they are almost always thinking about pornography and their level of involvement is extremely high. When clients seek help in the early stages of involvement in pornography (levels 1–4) it is generally because what they are seeing and experiencing is starting to concern them. They are concerned about where their behavior is headed if they do not course correct. This personal awareness is a contributor to why they are at lower levels of pornography addiction.

As you review each level of pornography addiction and involvement, you can see the progressive nature. Each level has unique characteristics. The jump from one level to the next is really based on the increase in frequency of finding and viewing pornography. It is also based on fantasizing, feelings of being out of control, and an increase in risk and potentially negative consequences.

Here are some questions for you to ask yourself.

- What is the highest level of pornography involvement in which you have been engaged in the last year?
- Which level of involvement most accurately describes your behaviors?

- When you are at higher levels, what is happening in your life? (For example, what is happening in your relationships, your family, job, etc.)
- How have you moved from a higher level to a lower level of involvement?

With a better understanding of your personal level of involvement, the next step is to assess the outcome or consequences of your pornography viewing habits. This is usually hard to do because heavy involvement in pornography can cause a person to lose touch with reality and how his actions are impacting others.

ASSESSING THE CONSEQUENCES

Only you will ever know the true depth of how pornography has impacted your mind and life. However, the truth may not even be manifest to you until you are able to honestly look at all of the consequences of pornography in your life. If a window into your life could be opened up for you to see the areas where you suffer because of pornography, what would you see? As you carefully consider each of the areas listed below, be honest in your evaluation. As you are honest your awareness will increase and you will understand more fully the seductive power pornography has had on you. Consider how pornography impacts the following areas in your life:

- Emotionally
- In relationships
- With your family
- Socially
- Spiritually
- Financially
- At work or school
- When facing withdrawal symptoms
- Sexually

When pornography turns into an addiction it is common for each of these areas to be influenced by its insidious effects. What is often overlooked while entrapped in the web of pornography is the influence it has in all aspects of one's life. In the following pages you will be given the opportunity to identify how pornography is influencing each of the areas listed above.

EMOTIONALLY

Our emotions are heavily influenced by the chemicals that run through our bodies. Consequently, when the pornography addict is viewing pornography he is altering his normal emotional state. At higher levels of pornography addiction, the addict's mind is used to endorphins being in the system. The endorphins numb the mind and create an emotional state similar to the high a drug addict would get. When a pornography addict comes down off the rush from the chemicals dumped into the system, he is likely to feel more depressed and emotionally down. This pattern can contribute to a relapse, since turning back to pornography can return the high. Also, when addicts attempt to go for extended periods of time without pornography, their minds can develop a craving for that feeling. As a result, pornography can alter the brain chemistry, leaving an addict feeling down, irritated, or on edge when not viewing pornography, and up and stimulated while viewing it.

Exercise 7: *Based on the information above, identify how pornography has influenced your emotions.*

Exercise 8: *List at least three emotions that are common for you to feel when thinking about pornography or while viewing it.*

Exercise 9: *What emotions do you feel before viewing pornography?*

Exercise 10: *What emotions do you feel after viewing pornography?*

IN RELATIONSHIPS

One of the common statements I hear from individuals struggling with pornography addiction is how much it impacts their relationships. Single clients generally take one of three approaches. The first group tells me they intentionally hold back in relationships because they don't feel good enough or worthy to be with the women around them. Those in the second group do not feel this same restraint and find they really want a relationship because they think it will help them fill the emptiness inside. The third group is sexually acting out and pornography is simply one of the ways that they act out sexually.

Pornography users in relationships also fit into different groups. Those in the first group have tried to get their spouses to view pornography with them. At times this works, but more often than not the spouse or partner doesn't want pornography to be a part of the relationship. Members of the second group keep their pornography viewing actions a secret and do not tell their spouse or partner. This secret inevitably hurts the trust and intimacy in the relationship.

One of the biggest challenges pornography presents in relationships is the lack of trust it creates. It hurts the feelings of loyalty and commitment the partners feel toward each other. It is common for spouses and partners of the addict to feel like there is something wrong with them. Often they try various behaviors to get their partner focused back on them. The spouse may even push her own sexual comfort zone in an effort to please her partner sexually. In many instances, feelings of betrayal, anger, hurt, and deceit lead to conflict and tension in the relationship.

Below you will find a few questions to help you identify how viewing pornography has impacted your relationships.

Exercise 11: *Identify the specific ways pornography has impacted your relationships.*

Exercise 12: *How has pornography impacted how you act in relationships?*

Exercise 13: *How has pornography impacted the people with whom you have relationships?*

WITH YOUR FAMILY

Seldom does pornography impact just one person. In many instances it influences all family members in one way or the other. This is especially true for individuals who are at higher levels of addiction. The pornography addict often becomes so focused on self that others and their needs are neglected. One client said, "I couldn't be a good dad because I couldn't get my mind off sexual images and experiences I had been having." When pornography is dominating the mind, family members often carry the brunt of the unavailable spouse or parent.

In the following assignments you will be asked to identify how pornography has impacted your family. This assignment is not easy because this is where you have likely created the most pain. After all, these are the people whom you care about most.

Exercise 14: *List five ways your family has been influenced by your involvement with pornography.*

Exercise 15: *If your family does not know that you are involved with pornography, is there a way you could share with them your struggle and utilize them as a resource to help you overcome this struggle? Write down your answer whether your answer is yes or no.*

Exercise 16: *In what ways has your family had to sacrifice because of your involvement with pornography?*

SOCIALLY

In social circumstances pornography-addicted clients are likely to do one of three things. The first possibility is that they will limit their social interaction. This often leads to further isolation and feelings of being alone. It has been hypothesized that social isolation can reduce a person's mental health. Many years ago a sociologist postulated that there was a critical number of social contacts a person needed every week to stay sane. He speculated that unless seven familiar people interacted with the person, he or she would be at risk for mental illness.[3]

Others turn social interaction into a search for sexual experiences. In these circumstances the entire purpose of socializing is to find an opportunity to act out sexually. In these circumstances, the social interaction can be dangerous (e.g., emotional issues and sexually transmitted diseases) and will seldom if ever lead to real or lasting relationships.

Those in the final group try to remain socially active. They attempt to interact with others and they have fun. However, they often limit how close others can get to them because they are afraid that if they get too close they will end up hurting the person. This happens because they don't feel like they have control over their addiction and they don't want to get hurt or hurt someone else. The consequence is that they try to have relationships but they aren't able to fully engage in them because of their addiction.

> **Exercise 17:** *Identify how pornography has impacted your social life. Then write down specific incidents when pornography impacted you socially.*

> **Exercise 18:** *If you are socially isolating yourself, what can you do to improve in this area? Write down some specific things that could change your current approach to social relationships.*

> **Exercise 19:** *If your social interaction is for the purpose of finding a sexual experience, what will you do to stop this behavior and develop more healthy social interactions? Write down some specific things you could do to change your current approach.*

SPIRITUALLY

When pornography addiction is at its worst, the role of spirituality in a person's life diminishes quickly. Most individuals who are struggling with a pornography addiction question their own spiritual beliefs. Some question whether God cares about them anymore. Others have stopped believing in God. Still others feel so ashamed and guilty that they stop attending religious services. The travesty of this is that spiritual emptiness and hopelessness often leads to extended relapses and strong bouts with depression, irritability, agitation, and other negative feelings.

When individuals become involved in a twelve-step process, such as in programs like Alcoholics Anonymous, they tap into their relationship with God. This relationship can be a great strength during the most challenging times of withdrawal and hopelessness. Inevitably, all people who struggle with pornography come to a conclusion about their relationship with God. When they turn toward God they find added capacity and strength to fight their inner battles and addiction.

> **Exercise 20**: *Identify how pornography has impacted your spirituality. Are there specific beliefs you have about God that have changed due to your involvement with pornography? If yes, please explain.*

> **Exercise 21**: *If you are a spiritual person, have you attempted to include God in your treatment plan? If so, write down how you have done this. If not, write down some things you can do to include God in your game plan.*

FINANCIALLY

When pornography addicts are binging it is common for them to spend money they do not have on pornography. They often minimize how much they are spending or how much pornography they are accumulating. When addicts have a stash of pornography and their behavior is still a secret, they generally try to find a hiding place. If this stash is found by a spouse it is often the beginning of the end of the relationship, as it destroys trust and confidence. If a child finds this stash, the child's curiosity can lead him to a lifetime of addiction as well.

With the increase in Internet usage there are less pornography stashes found in garages or other hidden areas and more pornographic images and videos that have been downloaded and saved on the computer hard drive. In a recent court case in which a man was accused and found guilty of sexual abuse of a child, the authorities found thousands of pornographic images on his computer and this contributed to the case against him. Ultimately, his stash was found in his hard drive. While accumulating stashes of pornography, thousands of dollars are spent to maintain and feed the addiction. Each year the amount of money spent on pornography grows exponentially. The statistical report for 2003 found that worldwide 56 billion dollars was spent on pornography during that year and 13 billion of that was spent in the United States[4]. Such numbers will only increase as pornography addiction increases.

The challenge of it all is that many addicts are spending money that they simply don't have. One man reported that while he was binging he would spend money on pornography rather than on food. Ultimately, when he had to make a choice as to whether he should eat or purchase access to a pornography website, he chose the pornography. The power and pull of pornography can make a rational man make decisions that seem ludicrous to the observer.

> **Exercise 22**: *How much money have you spent on pornography in the last year? Take some time and seriously evaluate how much you are spending each month. How is this addiction impacting your finances?*

> **Exercise 23**: *Do you have a stash of pornography? If so, how will the people you care most about react when they find it? How much money have you spent accumulating your stash? If that money had been invested, how much would it be worth today?*

AT WORK OR SCHOOL

People addicted to pornography often have challenges focusing at work or school. This is especially true when they have recently been viewing pornography. They often come to work late or tired because they stayed up all hours of the night. One man said it this way, "I would stay up late just so I could be by myself and view pornography. The time went so fast that I was only sleeping two or three hours a night. I was always tired, but I couldn't stop." In situations like this, work or school cannot be the focus. It is also common for the addicted person to spend time at work thinking or fantasizing about images seen the night before, or his mind starts planning his next episode.

It is not uncommon for individuals caught in this trap to lose their job or be passed over for promotions because of their problem with pornography. One person told me that he had been passed over for numerous advancements in his company because he had fallen asleep in a meeting. Another person told me that he had attended his college classes but was sleeping through them. As a result, his grades were dropping and he was afraid that he was going to fail all his classes.

When considering the cost of pornography we must take into consideration the things that are not accomplished. How much more effective would the person struggling to overcome a pornography addiction be if he was going to bed earlier? Or how much more effective would a student or employee be at school or work? What is the cost of this lost time to the employer or the college student who fails classes because of this addiction? What is the cost of replacing an employee who is viewing pornography at work? The cost of time is a lost resource that can never be reclaimed. Therefore, when evaluating the cost of pornography, we severely underestimate the real financial cost.

Exercise 24: *How has pornography impacted your effectiveness in accomplishing tasks at work or school? Describe in detail one or two experiences of how it has prevented you from being productive. The purpose of describing an experience is to help you honestly evaluate the true impact pornography has on you.*

Exercise 25: *What rules can you create to help you eliminate behaviors that prevent productivity at work or school? Ultimately, part of the healing process will be learning to be more productive at work or school.*

Example: *I will go to bed by midnight every work or school night. This is the rule that I must give myself if I am going to be able to function at work or school. I am going to accomplish this by setting my alarm to ring at 11:30 P.M. every night as a reminder that I need to start preparing for bed. The TV and computer will be turned off at 11:00 P.M. as a rule.*

WHEN FACING WITHDRAWAL SYMPTOMS

For those who question whether pornography is addictive, they need to only ask someone who has been addicted to pornography. Pornography addicts may not even be aware of the symptoms themselves. It is always interesting to hear my clients' responses when I ask them if they are experiencing any withdrawals. Many of them overlook the symptoms of withdrawal such as: insomnia, irritability, jitters, itchy skin, or genital discomfort or pain. When asked about these symptoms the pornography addicted person readily identifies with them. What is most challenging is that these withdrawal symptoms can last for two to eight weeks.[5]

Perhaps the biggest challenge of overcoming withdrawal symptoms is dealing with the emotions that accompany the withdrawal. Anytime a person goes through withdrawals there are both emotional and physical components that make it challenging. Since the withdrawal symptoms are so challenging, many addicts end up relapsing. For example, it is hard for the addicted person to know how to respond when he cannot sleep when he knows that if he gives in he will be able to fall asleep more readily.

Basically, there are two important parts to understanding withdrawal symptoms. First, each person must realize and identify his personal withdrawal symptoms. Second, he needs to create a plan of action regarding what he will do when he is feeling the withdrawal symptoms. It is important for each individual to identify his withdrawal symptoms because awareness is a big part of the recovery process.

Withdrawal is something each addict must go through. Few people realize that pornography creates a strong craving inside the mind. Those who have fought the battle readily admit it is one of the most difficult things that they have had to do in their life. However, these same individuals feel that overcoming that craving is one of the best things they have accomplished in their life. *The Sex and Love Addicts Anonymous* "Big Book" describes withdrawal this way.

> We cannot go through your withdrawal for you, nor would we, if we could. Who would ever knowingly volunteer to go through it again? Certainly none of us! Yet the pain of each withdrawal is unique and special, even precious (although you probably don't now think so). In a sense, the experience is you, a part of you which has been trying to surface for a long time. You have been avoiding or postponing this pain for a long time now, yet you have never been able to lastingly outrun it. You need to go through withdrawal in order to become a whole person. You need to meet yourself. Behind the terror of what you fear, withdrawal contains the seeds for your own personal wholeness. It must be experienced for you to realize, or make real, that potential for you and your life which has been stored there for so long.[6]

Exercise 26: *Write down the withdrawal symptoms you experience. If you need a list to compare with, consider the following:*
> *a. dizziness*
> *b. body aches*
> *c. headaches*
> *d. sleeplessness*
> *e. restlessness*
> *f. anxiety*
> *g. mood swings*

Exercise 27: *Make a list of things you can do to counter your withdrawal symptoms. This list needs to be full of ideas and behaviors* *that you are committed to doing. If you won't do it when you are struggling through withdrawal, do not write it down.*

SEXUALLY

Some experts believe viewing erotic material enhances the sexual experience. However, for the pornography addict erotic material will actually take away the fulfilling depth of legitimate sexual intimacy. Pornography impacts a person's view of sex in many ways. It can warp a person's perception of what a healthy sexual relationship is like. Consider the following story. Aaron was a good friend of mine who unbeknownst to me was addicted to pornography. One night while talking about his marriage he asked me what he should do when his wife didn't want to have oral or anal sex. He thought she should have no problem with that. A few months later his wife found him on an Internet chat site having an online affair. His mind had been so altered by the pornography that he was viewing that he thought something was wrong with his wife when she wouldn't perform those acts with him. He consequently sought out opportunities to act out his fantasies.

This story is but one of thousands and thousands of stories of how pornography can alter the mind. When a couple struggles with different approaches to sexuality in the relationship, the relationship is in a very dangerous place. Sex therapists have often said that a couple's sex life is like a window into the rest of their relationship. If this is true, when one spouse views his or her partner as a sexual object to experiment with, the vain ambitions will lead to hurt and anguish.

In addition, constant viewing of pornography can actually lead to a sexual relationship that is not fulfilling for either partner. The addict will not be satisfied with the frequency, and as result often turns to pornography and masturbation to fulfill his high sex drive. The partner who is not involved is more likely to withdraw and feel uncomfortable having sex. Women have told me that this is because they feel used, dirty, or uncomfortable because they know they aren't as physically attractive as the porn stars.

Exercise 28: *Write down how pornography has altered your perception of sex. Has it changed your perception of what is physically attractive to you?*

Exercise 29: *How has pornography impacted your sexual behaviors? Are there times when viewing pornography reduces the amount of sex you have with your partner? Have you chosen to view pornography rather than have sex with your partner?*

Exercise 30: *What are some of the steps you can take to find a healthy sexual relationship?*

Example: *By stopping my viewing of pornography and the high I get from it, I will try to identify more with my partner. I will have more love and compassion for her by trying to understand her and her desires.*

Chapter 3:
Pornography Unveiled—Why Pornography is Addictive and How to Activate and Deactivate Addictive Behaviors

I have learned that treating pornography addiction is hard. I am a professional who has seen grown men and women cry because they cannot stop looking at pornography. They tell themselves over and over that "this will be the last time," only to give in a few hours, days, weeks, or months later. After repeatedly giving in and breaking the barriers that they have erected to prevent a slip-up they begin to feel hopeless. Often their own despair leads them into relapse. Many are devastated because they promised their spouse, their religious leader, or their therapist that they were done.

For those addicted, viewing pornography is a vicious cycle. They commit and recommit to stop looking at pornography, then after time their resolve weakens and they become more vulnerable. They experience stress, frustration, fear, anger, and myriad other emotions. Amidst these painful emotions, the only way they have found peace of mind in the past is to give in and view pornography. Sometimes they will fantasize for hours at a time in an effort to avoid the reality of their life. Unfortunately, not only has pornography become the chosen comforting element in their life, it is extremely addictive.

Dr. Patrick Carnes, a renowned sexual addiction counselor, reported in his research with over 1,000 individuals that sex addiction is more challenging to overcome than drugs or alcohol. Dr. Carnes writes, "We have learned that addictive obsession can exist in whatever generates significant mood alteration, whether it be the self-nurturing of food, the excitement of gambling, or the arousal of seduction. One of the more destructive parts of sex addiction is that you literally carry your own source of supply."[1] What this means is that the brain naturally produces chemicals. Unlike any drug or alcohol substance, our own internal chemistry produces the addictive chemicals while viewing pornography, and these chemicals are very addictive when they are abused. We can get high on our own internal brain chemicals.

The specific chemicals include: epinephrine, testosterone, endorphins (endogenous morphine), oxytocin (a bonding peptide strongly associated with feelings of love), dopamine, serotonin, and phenlethylamine.[2] While these chemicals have multiple purposes, researchers have found that they parallel the molecular structure of amphetamines, which create a high-arousal state. Once released, these chemicals have an immediate effect on the mind and body, but are relatively short lived. Thus, the addicted individual will often begin repeating the cycle over and over again to maintain the high that comes with viewing pornography. In the process of maintaining the high, he alters the chemical make up of the brain.

Dr. Carnes writes, "Prolonged use alters these individuals' brain chemistry until they 'require' the excitement in order to feel 'normal.'" The battle of overcoming pornography is further complicated by masturbation. In over one hundred cases involving people I have personally met with, only three have not associated pornography and masturbation, and these individuals had minimal exposure to pornography. When pornography and masturbation are at work together, the mind is receiving an incredible amount of chemicals. The excitement and high are exhilarating to the addict.

One of the chemicals released by the brain is endorphins. Researchers Harvey B. Milkman and Stanley Sunderwirth found that, "endorphins (and the limbic system) must somehow be involved in the ecstasy of sexual activity and orgasm."[3] As the mind develops a desire for these powerful chemicals, the body realizes it can tap into this source anytime it wants to. Thus, the addicted individual can create an endorphin high on the spur of the moment. Some clients have told me that they get high simply by fantasizing about the images that they have seen.

Competing with these internal chemicals is not easy, primarily because most individuals cannot imagine life without them. They are more prone to feel "normal" only when they are viewing pornography. They go through emotionally painful withdrawals when they attempt to stop looking at pornography. This is why the addicted person often returns to the behavior time and time again. The battle is a hard one. Sadly, most addicts don't seek help until they are far down the pathway headed toward destruction. They wait until they have lost friends, relationships, their job, or a scholarship.

If you have lost something of value to you or if you are fortunate enough to have recognized that a problem exists before something significant happens, now is the time to understand what is happening inside of you so you can change this addictive process. The following section will help you understand how your addiction developed and how you can learn to break out of this process before it gets deeply rooted in your mind's pathways.

THE DEVELOPMENT OF ADDICTION IN THE HUMAN MIND

One way to understand how an addiction develops in the brain is to learn how a reaction sequence is created. A reaction sequence is a pathway formed in the mind that generally begins with a stimulus and ends with a specific response. Once developed, a reaction sequence will automatically change a person's emotional state. An example of this comes from a personal experience I had as boy. A boy moved into my neighborhood and I decided to visit him. On my way up to his house his dog came out and bit me on the leg. Since then, every time I hear a dog bark (stimulus) I automatically become tense and uptight (response) until I can rationally think through what is happening.

In applying this to pornography, consider how this could lead to the development of an addiction. The first time people see pornography their minds don't necessarily understand the stimulus that triggers strong emotions and feelings, but they generally like the feeling. However, the next time they view pornography, it is no longer a novelty and they know the emotions they experience while viewing pornography. Over time a person can associate these feelings with finding comfort when under stress or lonely. It can provide a quick fix when a person is looking for something to do when bored. Thus, the human mind, with more exposure, elevates the need or demand for such strong feelings. These strong emotions are accompanied by the release of chemicals inside the brain. These chemicals (as described earlier) are very addictive.

Another critical point to consider is that just thoughts or memories of pornography can trigger emotions. For example, Terry Robinson of the University of Michigan described what happens to drug addicts on a subconscious level when he wrote, "Crack pipes, syringes, the sound of ice tinkling in a glass full of scotch can act as cues that induce craving much like the sound of a bell caused Pavlov's dogs to salivate. Even though addicts can become conscious of the relationship between some drug-related cues and their craving . . . they might not recognize that a certain place or smell wakens a hunger for the drug."[4] With this in mind, the focus should turn toward learning how to recognize as many triggers as possible so that the reaction sequences can be understood and deactivated. This will be described in the section to follow.

However, before introducing the development of a reaction sequence it is important to mention that there are many triggers that may cause a person to want to view pornography. The availability of pornography or sexual images is staggering. Consider that sexual images can be seen on TV, in movies, on billboards, via the Internet, in magazines, and in how people dress. With all of the possible ways to get exposure, it is virtually impossible to completely cut off all of the triggers. However, preparing to stop them before emotions become too high can help in recovery.

Here is the entire reaction sequence as it relates to pornography.

Stimulus (trigger)—See a pornographic magazine, or view an email that comes to your inbox with pornographic image or link. There are hundreds of potential stimuli that get the mind thinking about pornography; our society doesn't help much with this.

Once the stimulus is triggered in the mind the next thing that happens is that our mind gives meaning to the stimulus. The first thing a person will do is have an emotional response.

Emotion—Instant excitement, interest, or curiosity are common emotions.

Almost simultaneous to the emotions being felt is a thought in the mind.

Thought—Initially the thought may be "I wonder" or "What will I see or find." Once this initial interest and curiosity settles in, the thought is likely to be something like, "I could look at pornography" or "I like what I am feeling—why not?"

When the emotion and thought of viewing pornography are entertained, the mind quickly begins to release chemicals into the body in anticipation of what is going to happen next.

Chemical Release—The body is flooded with chemicals preparing the body for what it will see and what could happen. It is important to note that once a reaction sequence is fully developed in the mind, these chemicals are released into the body before a person ever sees pornography.

With the release of these chemicals into the body, the body begins to change.

Body Language—A person's heart rate will increase; his hands may become sweaty or cold. His eyes will likely become dilated. The muscles become tight or rigid.

With the body feeling strong emotions, the mind still has to decide if it is going to give in and view pornography or not. This is when the more rational part of the mind steps in and says, "Are you sure you want to do this?" It is the mind's back-up system that allows it to respond rather than react every time.

Thought—This second thought is what I call the battle. The battle inside goes something like this:

I really shouldn't look at pornography.
What will my wife think?
What if I get caught?
I could lose my job.

While these thoughts are going on, the mind is also thinking:

I have been doing this for years, what's one more time going to matter?
I deserve this.
It's not that big of a deal.
Nobody will find out.

Unfortunately, most individuals wait too long before this battle begins and the mind has already released the chemicals into the body, thus making the battle a very hard one to fight. Ultimately the winning thoughts of this battle determine the outcome. The battle comes to an end when the mind authorizes a specific behavior. The authorizing agent is generally a hypothesis or a belief (a hypothesis is a thought that is not cemented into the mind, whereas a belief is something that you truly believe). *Hypothesis/Belief*—I wonder if this will ever go away (hypothesis). Common beliefs include: I cannot get over this problem so why try? I deserve this. It isn't that bad. One more time won't hurt.

Before a person views pornography he must first accept the behavior as something that is okay. Therefore, the authorization from the beliefs is a very important part of this process. *Response*—The most common response at this point is giving in and viewing pornography, which will likely end in masturbation.

Once a reaction sequence has been established in the mind it can take a matter of seconds to go through the whole process described above. That is why so many people claim they feel they have no control over their compulsive behavior. Unfortunately, too much stimuli can lead to multiple reaction sequences in people, and that, if left undealt with, creates a high probability for relapse. One of the reasons pornography is so dangerous is that the mind can run through a reaction sequence simply by fantasizing about previous images that have been viewed.

DEACTIVATING A REACTION SEQUENCE—THE FIRST STEP TO BREAKING AN ADDICTION

What is exciting is that reaction sequences can be changed or deactivated. Deactivating a reaction sequence requires an individual to first understand his own reaction sequence. Then, the next time it happens the individual must realize it is happening as quickly as possible—early awareness is critical. Finally, he must create a new response when the reaction sequence begins. A reaction sequence that is never evaluated or understood will lead to the same behaviors over and over again.

Here is a story that illustrates the steps that can be taken to deactivate a reaction sequence. John had been dealing with a sexual addiction for many years. In the process of working with him I outlined the reaction sequence and together we worked on rewriting his reaction sequence. A few weeks later he came to my office very excited. He shared with me that while attending a meeting with a woman he was interested in, his reaction sequence started when she was invited by some other friends to attend the next meeting. But when she didn't introduce him to her friends, he felt rejected. He felt like he wasn't part of their group. At this point, John told me that his normal response would be to go and find something that would be sexually stimulating to him. However, when he chose to go and read a book instead of seeking out sexual stimulation, he altered his most common response— seeking a sexual experience.

The moment people gain awareness into their own reaction sequences they are more likely to understand themselves. This awareness is a good starting point for creating change. Therefore, in my work as a therapist I ask my clients to outline their own reaction sequences. Here's a picture one of my clients created as he outlined his own reaction sequence.

GRAPH 1: REACTION SEQUENCE

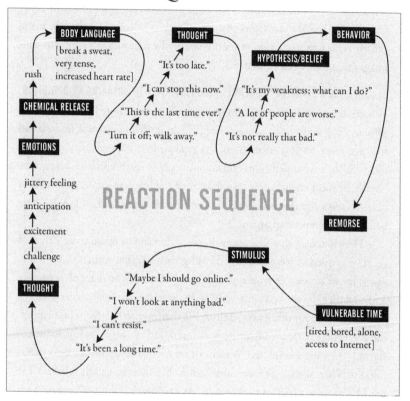

Starting at the bottom right hand side you will see the beginning of this client's reaction sequence. He started by outlining the times he was most vulnerable. Then he continued along the bottom of the page to the stimulus. You can track his reaction sequence by following the arrows. There is a place to diagram reaction sequences in Appendix A.

Once the reaction sequence is outlined and understood it is a good idea to review the sequence over and over until it can be recognized each time a stimulus starts. Many clients have told me that understanding their own reaction sequence has helped them gain awareness, and then with this awareness they are able to do something different.

However, awareness of a reaction sequence means very little if the next step of creating a game plan and acting upon that plan is ignored. The deactivation of a reaction sequence requires a good game plan that can be used to break negative thought patterns or behaviors. A game plan can help deactivate the reaction sequences and help create new ways of acting rather than acting out. Here's an example of a game plan.

GRAPH 2: THE GAME PLAN

A game plan includes the following steps:

1. Write down the behavior that you want to change. Be as specific as possible. For example: I want to stop looking at pornography. Pornography includes: magazines, Internet images, and will also include images of women in swimsuits.
2. Write down the reaction sequence that leads to the behavior you want to change (as seen in Graph 1—Also see Appendix A where you can map out your own reaction sequence).
3. Write down the specific behaviors you will change in each part of the reaction sequence. For example, this client focused on reducing the times he was vulnerable (as seen on the bottom right hand corner of Graph 2). Writing down the vulnerable moments helps identify the specific thoughts, feelings, and experiences that contribute to relapsing. He also worked on stopping the thoughts such as "Maybe I should go online." Next he attempted to reduce the strong emotions by doing alternative activities such as going to the store, reading a book, or calling a friend.
4. The next step is to review the game plan each time the reaction sequence runs to determine whether it has been successful or not.

In addition to developing a game plan there are other lessons that can be learned from deactivating a reaction sequence. Below are some exercises.

Exercise 31: *Write down the times you are most vulnerable to giving in to pornography.*

Exercise 32: *Turn to Appendix A and write down each of the steps of your reaction sequence.*

Exercise 33: *Spend extra time writing down all of the beliefs that you have that authorize you to view pornography.*

Example: *When I get into an argument with my wife/girlfriend I believe I am justified in viewing pornography.*

Tremendous value and insight can be gained from identifying your reaction sequence and writing down a game plan. The awareness you gain can help you overcome addictive behaviors. When a game plan includes new behaviors and positive rewards, the addictive cycle can be broken. Creating a game plan helps develop a stronger foundation so that change can begin to occur. The next chapter focuses on the power of beliefs that prevent growth and change.

Chapter 4:
The Power of Beliefs—Learn to Rewrite the Beliefs That Keep You Trapped

It is a common practice in our society to focus on misbehavior (e.g., addiction, anger, and abuse) rather than getting to the root of the problem. Most attempts at changing misbehaviors are centered on stopping the behavior. With addictions, getting to the root needs to be the central component before true healing and change can occur. However, if there is no understanding of why the misbehavior occurred in the first place, the intervention to stop the behavior will likely fail. It is like putting a band-aid on an infected wound without first cleaning it. True change only occurs when thoughts or beliefs that guide misbehaviors are changed.

To illustrate this point, consider the story of 17-year-old Steve who went to his religious leader to confess viewing pornographic magazines, X-rated videos, and Internet pornography. His leader discussed how bad such behaviors were, but never gave encouragement to Steve—simply told him to stop viewing pornography and never go back again. After repeated discussions and countless relapses, Steve gave up trying. He avoided his leader because he felt guilty inside. He felt like a failure because he couldn't stop on his own. Soon he was withdrawing from others. He believed all was helpless and hopeless.

When Steve came into my office he told me I was his last resort. He said, "I have tried everything and I am sick of trying." Over the next few weeks he and I discussed much of the material from the first three chapters of this book. He gained a great amount of awareness into his addiction and the power of pornography. He learned how pornography becomes addictive to the mind and how it can alter the mind. He began to realize that stopping pornography in his life required gaining extra knowledge and a keen awareness of self. He also learned that pornography is not something that is simply overcome through exerting strong willpower. Finally, he learned that overcoming his addiction was a process and not an event. Only when Steve learned these things did his negative beliefs about himself and his addiction begin to change.

Steve related to me how he had begun to doubt himself. He reported that he was once vibrant and full of energy—he had loved life. Now he could not imagine life without pornography. He was so ashamed of his behaviors that he had isolated himself from his close friends and even his family was kept at a distance. In the process of gaining awareness into his thoughts and beliefs he learned about the power of his beliefs. He had formed so many negative beliefs about himself that they fueled his relapses. His beliefs about himself had truly kept him trapped for many years. His beliefs were feeding into his addiction. Some of his key beliefs were:

- I'm alone and nobody understands how hard I am trying but I cannot stop.
- Nobody has problems like me.
- I deserve what I get since I am not strong enough to quit on my own.
- I am a bad person.
- Nobody will want me.
- I cannot meet my family's expectations.

Such beliefs kept Steve in a trap. He didn't realize this until he wrote them down and saw the thoughts that were guiding his day to day living. When we discussed his beliefs he realized how they had been guiding his life. He wrote them down one by one and began challenging them.

CHALLENGING UNHEALTHY BELIEFS

The process of challenging beliefs is not hard to do once a person recognizes the beliefs that are guiding his behavior and then goes through the following steps. The first step for Steve was to realize his belief and write it down.

"No one else has problems like me."

Once he realized that this was his guiding belief, I asked him to provide me with all of the evidence he could that supported this statement (this was step two).

His list included:

- I have been dealing with this for years and others can quit anytime.
- I don't have strong willpower like others.
- I have repeatedly told myself that I would not relapse again but I keep going back to it.

Notice that these statements are also beliefs. The third step in challenging unhealthy beliefs for Steve was to give all the evidence he could that might suggest this statement was not true. This took some time as Steve had never before questioned whether his beliefs were true or false. This step almost always creates a new perspective. Many of my clients have never questioned whether their beliefs were accurate or inaccurate. In Steve's case this was the turning point. He had just assumed that he was alone and that there must be something seriously wrong with him. Once he realized that his beliefs might be wrong, the fun began.

He started by asking me how many people I had seen who were dealing with pornography addiction. When I told him over one hundred he realized he wasn't alone. Then he thought about how big of an industry pornography is and how much money it generates each year (over $56 billion annually). As he looked at these thoughts, he realized that millions of others were also struggling with pornography. This helped him realize that he was surely not alone in his battle with pornography.

In the fourth step I asked Steve to examine how these beliefs had affected him. This information was easily accessed by reviewing what he had been doing socially and with his family. He was able to identify that his beliefs had prevented him from getting close to the women he dated and he avoided his family and friends when he was heavily involved in pornography. Such actions led him to increased feelings of being alone and of isolation. The process of examining the impact broadened his self-understanding. He learned that a single belief had the capacity to affect his entire life.

Once through the first four stages, the final stage is much easier. In step five Steve created a game plan so that the next time his negative belief tried to sneak its way into his mind, he quickly challenged it to reflect the new information and insight he had gained. Anytime a person creates a game plan he should include specific things that he will do the next time he begins to feel those negative thoughts and feelings. Here is a short list of things I recommend to clients:

Create a protective barrier to remind you not to accept those negative thoughts (e.g., write down reminders on mirrors or refrigerator doors). You may want to adopt a phrase that we teach people who come through our classes, "I don't need to go there!" meaning, "I am not going to let this negative thought overtake my thinking."

Be emotionally honest with yourself. Having already looked at the belief, you know the truth. By allowing yourself to keep going back to the same negative thoughts you are ignoring what you have previously learned.

Develop new thoughts so that the next time you begin to feel that way you have other thoughts to play in your mind. Some of the things you might consider doing include: memorize something, create as many positive thoughts as you can to replace the negative beliefs, or call a friend so that your mind doesn't keep thinking the same negative thoughts.

Include a friend in your game plan. A support system offers strength when you may need it the most. Some negative beliefs are so powerful that only friends or family can give us a reality check.

Exercise 34: *Go through the following steps to help you understand and overcome old belief patterns.*

1. Write down the beliefs you have about yourself, your relationships, and others, that are a direct result of your involvement with pornography.
2. Provide as much evidence as you can that supports your beliefs.
3. Look at your beliefs and ask whether there is any evidence that would make the belief false or true.
4. Identify how your beliefs have impacted you. Be specific.
5. Create a plan of action for the next time this belief comes into your mind.

When you have looked at your beliefs, why you believe what you believe, and how your beliefs have impacted you, and then take the final step of making a plan of action, these things will help you break the negative beliefs you have accepted as truth. The process of challenging negative beliefs is very effective for those who are willing to go through this learning exercise. In many instances new hope is found and motivation increases to help fight the battle.

MOTIVATION

When people begin to look at their problems as if they can be solved, a new and positive feeling comes upon them. This is when positive change is just around the corner. When Steve realized he wasn't alone, his hope soared and he began talking like he was going to win his battle with pornography. This hope increased his motivation. Until motivation levels are high it is almost impossible to create the necessary change it requires to stop looking at pornography. Pornography is hard to overcome, but when there is no motivation, change will not happen. Motivation comes when individuals begin to see their problem as something that can be solved.

Researchers have consistently explored what works and what does not when treating addicts. The findings suggest that effective approaches instill within the client the belief that he can change. With a belief that change is possible, motivation increases and the addict learns to utilize his own strengths. Here are some additional methods that can be used to increase motivation for change.

- Look at and identify beliefs that keep you trapped in negative behaviors.
- Realize that you have the seeds to the solutions of your problems within you.
- Seek new knowledge or skills.
- Use your own values to help you change.
- Check your progress over time, but do not force the desired changes upon yourself.

Each of these methods will be described below.

LOOK AT AND IDENTIFY BELIEFS THAT KEEP YOU TRAPPED IN NEGATIVE BEHAVIORS

As you look at the example of Steve you can readily see that his change started as a direct result of feeling hope again. I believe this does not happen without evaluation of the beliefs that keep you trapped. Only when these beliefs are challenged do new options seem possible. One client put it this way, "I hadn't felt any hope for many months; now that I see how all of my beliefs have prevented me from being social, relating with my family, and doing well at work, I feel free."

Our beliefs are very powerful because they guide our behaviors. For example, as part of the reaction sequence described in chapter three, assignments were given to help you identify the beliefs that authorize you to view pornography. This is one of the most critical steps in the change process. As beliefs are evaluated it becomes obvious that they need to be reexamined. Some of the most common beliefs that I hear with pornography are:

- One more time won't hurt.

- I deserve it.
- This is just who I am.
- It is not that big of a deal.
- Everyone is doing it.

Once these beliefs are identified they often sound silly or ridiculous to the individual who has used them for reasons to view pornography. It is essential, however, that these beliefs are understood and evaluated. Then they need to be rewritten one at a time. Here is an example of how this could be done.

Belief: One more time won't hurt.

Reality: I have been saying this for many years now and it is never just one more time. What are the outcomes of telling myself that one more time won't hurt? I give in and feel bad. Then, because I have given in again, I binge for a few days and feel like all is helpless. So what will I do the next time I think "One more time won't hurt?" I am going to say out loud, "That isn't true." The truth is, one more time will hurt and I will have to start the recovery process over if I allow this thought to stay in my mind.

Since beliefs are often the authorizer of behaviors, it is imperative that beliefs are taken seriously if change is going to happen. As a therapist I have met with many people who have never thought about their beliefs. When they start asking themselves which beliefs authorize them to look at pornography, they learn a lot about themselves and why they are doing what they do.

In the process of looking at beliefs it is important to remember that you may have many beliefs that you have never verbalized before. Therefore, one good method of getting at your beliefs is to write them down on paper, making them more real and easier to challenge. It is a common occurrence that while writing down beliefs you will learn much about yourself and why you think and feel the way you do.

When beliefs are truly evaluated and challenged it is common to experience more hope, which in turn leads to an increase in motivation to change. Negative beliefs about self can be so overwhelming and can defeat motivation so thoroughly that when they are gone it is as if shackles had been removed after years of bondage.

REALIZE THAT YOU HAVE THE SEEDS TO THE SOLUTIONS OF YOUR PROBLEMS WITHIN YOU

Many of the best counselors have come to realize that therapy is most effective when clients come up with solutions on their own. However, when it comes to addiction, this can be a double-edged sword. Most addicts want to deal with their addiction on their own. They believe that they can handle their problems without someone telling them what to do or how to do it. Unfortunately, those who have such beliefs are the very ones who need the most help. On the other hand, researchers have found that most addicts actually do quit on their own.[1]

Most of us want to solve our own problems. Therefore, it is hard to admit to yourself and others that we cannot change without help. It takes a lot of courage and humility to admit addiction. Indeed, one of the biggest steps an addict can take in the recovery process is to admit an addiction exists. This is the first step to finding a solution. If a problem is not owned (seen as a problem), it cannot be solved. Consequently, those who heal the quickest are the ones who openly talk about and discuss their addiction.

In many instances, talking about misbehavior starts the change process. Then real lasting change occurs when individuals realize they have the ability within their own heart to alter their current behaviors. Stanley Arnold said, "Every problem contains the seeds of its own solution." In commenting on this, one client said, "When I realized that no one else could do this for me I began learning as much as I could about my addiction. I had no idea how freeing it would be to seek and find my own solutions. Obviously, I needed the help of others, but the buck had to stop with me." When this occurred the dark cloud that had overwhelmed this client lifted and the years of pain and frustration began to break. Hope emerged and a tinge of excitement came out.

Ultimately, when an individual realizes he has the solutions within himself, he feels freer. Most realize that they do not have what it takes on their own so they begin seeking new knowledge and information in books, groups, counselors, and other support systems. When the individual realizes the progress that can be made with the right tools and a clear understanding of self, he feels a strong desire to learn and develop new skills to make changes. This is the next part of motivation.

SEEK NEW KNOWLEDGE OR SKILLS

One of the most valuable lessons I have learned as a therapist is to gather more data when I don't have enough information. Without enough information, those who struggle with addiction can easily feel overwhelmed and out of control. When people who are battling pornography seek help, they are really looking for new ways or ideas they have not tried before. In instances like this education is very important. Many addicts have become so used to giving in that they question whether they can quit. Therefore, when I see clients who feel hopeless and helpless as a result of pornography addiction, I try to let them know that with more knowledge and skills they can overcome their addiction. Only when our minds can see a new way does it begin to feel hopeful.

There are skills that addicts can develop to overcome an addiction. With the right tools, not only is it possible to overcome addiction, but life can take on a whole new meaning. Some of the knowledge that has helped my clients break the feelings of hopelessness include:

- Learning how the mind developed the addiction
- An understanding of why pornography is so addictive
- The development of the reaction sequence

- Developing a specific game plan
- Reaching out and asking others for help
- Creating a new lifestyle
- Using personal values and beliefs to strengthen your resolve

When these skills have been developed and honed there is an internal power that begins to emerge and the addict begins to see that this addiction can be overcome. With the knowledge of how to implement these skills there is additional motivation to change for good.

USE YOUR OWN VALUES TO HELP YOU CHANGE

One of the biggest challenges of overcoming an addiction is to change your values or to realign them with previously established values. For example, have you wondered how viewing pornography fits in with your personal values? In today's society values and character are discussed more in passing than they are given serious attention. However, most people still have values they try to live by. These values are important to them and that is why so many people are struggling with their pornography addiction. It feels wrong, but because its pull is so strong it is common to violate one's own values to get a high from pornography.

The question that must be asked is "What values are guiding your life?" In his book *7 Tools to Break Addictive Behaviors*, Dr. Stanton Peele wrote, "In order to decide what recovery path to take, you must first understand what is important to you, what you believe, and what you consider to be right."[2] When this happens your internal compass can guide you to place your values as a high priority and can increase your motivation to change.

It has become a common practice of mine to ask clients why they want to change and in particular I want to know why *now*. One of the most common responses I receive is that they want to change because viewing pornography is not in line with their values. They feel guilty, ashamed, and out of control. Many just want to start thinking about new things and living a different lifestyle. They spend so much time thinking about or viewing pornography that their personal goals are starting to slip from their life. This is in direct conflict with the things that they value. Consequently, when they begin to heal, their behaviors begin focusing on things that they value. One man put it this way, "I just switched jobs. This is something that I would have never dared to do when I was so involved in my addiction." People feel freer when they allow their deep convictions and values guide their behaviors.

CHECK YOUR PROGRESS OVER TIME, BUT DO NOT FORCE THE DESIRED CHANGES UPON YOURSELF

Aaron had been working for many days to fend off the desire to return to pornography. He had carefully focused on living his life one day at a time, but his craving was not subsiding. Finally, after a couple of weeks of fighting the battle, he relapsed. He came to therapy very despondent. He had expected that he would be able to withstand the challenges and withdrawal symptoms no matter what. He was so focused on succeeding that when he did not fend off the craving, he lost his motivation to try. He binged for a few days and then reluctantly called to set up an appointment. Together we explored the relapse and he explained that he felt trapped by not being able to ever go back and view pornography. He felt like he had lost something; pornography was a part of him. In looking at his feelings he admitted he was trying to force everything to be perfect. He wanted to be over this battle with pornography so badly that he was trying to force everything to happen.

When change occurs it is generally a gradual process. There are circumstances where individuals go cold turkey but this is not the norm. Most people who quit an addiction take gradual steps that eventually lead to complete success. Therefore, it is important to monitor relapse patterns and identify when these patterns are broken. Edward is a perfect example of this. He had been binging daily for months and he had given up on overcoming his addiction. When he sought treatment he did not know if he could ever quit, but he thought he would at least try. After a few sessions he realized that overcoming pornography is not an event, it is a process that requires time, knowledge, the right tools, and a good support system. However, the most exciting element for Edward was when he learned to monitor his progress and success stories rather than whether he relapsed or not. He began monitoring his progress to the point that he was avoiding pornography weeks at a time. For him this was tremendous progress. It was freeing to him to realize that he could make progress. Over the next few months he worked on learning from each relapse. This further increased his motivation as he realized he could succeed, and eventually he believed he could stop completely. For most pornography addicts step-by-step progress is a better way of looking at recovery rather than an all-or-nothing approach.

There are many lessons we learn from those who have succeeded in overcoming an addiction. Perhaps the greatest lesson is that it requires motivation. If there is not motivation, the first step is to find a reason to get motivated. Once you have motivation, the next step is to find additional reasons to *keep* motivated. Then, using knowledge and new ideas, it is time to learn from mistakes and keep the attitude that this will not happen that day. Finally, identifying and using one's own belief and value system is a great method to stay motivated.

Chapter 5:
The Beginning Steps to Change for Good

"We change, whether we like it or not." —*Ralph Waldo Emerson*

If there is one concern most of my clients express, it is whether they can change for good. Many of them have recognized that they have a problem but they haven't found a way to stop viewing pornography. They have been dealing with pornography since childhood and they have told themselves over and over again that they were done viewing pornography, only to find themselves involved again. Change is intimidating and overwhelming to most people, but especially the addict.

After trying and failing so many times, it is easy to form a belief that change is either too much work or impossible to accomplish. Perhaps that is why so many people put their lives on autopilot and live for years without ever trying to change their behavior. Autopilot is a place the mind goes when it does not think it can solve a problem. We call this place safety. Safety is the place the mind goes just to survive.

Fortunately, with the right information and tools, living in safety is not necessary. Once given the right tools, change is not only possible but it is also exciting. It is exciting when you learn how to change and alter previously unacceptable behavior. Change, however, comes in stages. These stages were best described by Dr. Prochaska and his colleagues in their book *Changing for Good.*[1] Here they discuss six stages of change that will be discussed in this and the final chapters of this book. The six stages are:

- Precontemplation
- Contemplation
- Preparation

- Taking Action
- Maintenance
- Relapse Prevention

PRECONTEMPLATION

In the precontemplation stage most individuals don't believe their behavior is a problem. They may have periodic thoughts that they should change, but seldom do these thoughts last. They (as described earlier) are in safety. While in safety very little change occurs in a person's life. At this stage he does the same things over and over, often developing rituals or patterns that later, in the recovery process, become one of his biggest challenges.

Since the human mind likes predictability and consistency it quickly assimilates every experience it has and makes meaning of it. It develops habits and patterns as a matter of convenience and in order to simplify what it does. That is why so many people who are trying to break an addiction get frustrated when they have committed to themselves that they are done viewing pornography, but without really thinking about what they are doing, find themselves looking at it again. Once patterns are set in our mind it is easy to switch on the autopilot and perform the same behaviors repeatedly. This makes staying in the precontemplation stage a plausible option.

Another issue surrounding the precontemplation stage is that many people do not realize how hard it is to stop looking at pornography. Many of the people I have worked with have told me that for many years they thought they could stop their behavior at anytime. Then, when they try to quit for extended periods of time, they find it much harder than they imagined.

To further complicate matters our culture does not help remedy this situation. In fact, our media and various other outlets are pushing the boundaries with sexual content, trying to get our entire culture to openly accept various versions of pornography. As a result, the general population has come to accept sexual images as part of television, movies, or other media sources. The general public has become desensitized and does not consider these sexual images a problem. Indeed, it is difficult to see pornography as a problem when an entire population is accepting it.

Consequently, many people who exhibit behaviors associated with a pornography addiction do not consider that they may have a problem. They may not perceive viewing pornography at work or school as a problem. Or they may not see it as a problem that they prefer viewing pornography to being sexually intimate with their spouse. Such actions illustrate the pre-contemplation stage because no thought is given to how one's own actions impact others or that any change is needed. If there is a theme of this stage it is "there is no problem." Such is the mindset of the individual in the pre-contemplation stage.

However, most addicts do not stay in the precontemplation stage. They cannot. Their actions often escalate to the point that they feel guilty, ashamed, and out of control. Their actions are in violation of their own belief and value system. When this occurs people do one of two things. They either lower their standards to meet their actions (which keeps them in the precontemplation stage), or they work to improve their actions to meet their standards.

STANDARDS

ACTIONS

As long as an individual's standards and actions are not in harmony he will be in dissonance (stress). This is an emotionally hard place to be. These individuals have a hard time focusing at work, at home, in school, or with whatever tasks they are trying to accomplish. This is one of the key reasons why it is hard to stay in the precontemplation stage.

Another factor that often facilitates the need to change out of the precontemplation stage is getting caught by a spouse, parent, or employer. When this occurs the addict encounters a motivational crisis. Motivational crises are often key to getting individuals out of the status quo. While many addicts want to change, the majority of them do not until there is no other choice and they are backed into a corner. When a marriage, family, or job is on the line, contemplation for change quickly comes to the forefront.

CONTEMPLATION

During the contemplation stage addicts realize that change is needed; they are no longer in denial. However, they are still debating whether they want to change and whether they have the strength to change. This stage can last for weeks, months, or sometimes years depending on the reason the person chooses to change. In the field of counseling it has been theorized that change occurs for one of three reasons: fear, duty, and love. Let's explore each of these reasons and their contribution to the contemplation stage of change.

FEAR

When clients come to therapy out of fear they are generally motivated by an external source. In other words, the reason for change is coming from outside of self rather than being self imposed. Some of the reasons fear motivates a person to change are:

- Loss of spouse
- A family member caught them
- Fear of disappointing others
- Loss of job
- Social embarrassment
- Court ordered
- Punishment from God

Many addicts report that fear is an initial reason they seek help. While fear can be a good motivator to start the changing process, seldom is it given as the reason for long-term change. One client put it this way, "I was so upset when my mom caught me that I didn't dare look at pornography for many months afterwards." With fear guiding his actions, he eventually overcame the fear of being caught and tried to be sneakier. Eventually he learned how to avoid getting caught.

There are times when fear of losing something, such as a marriage, can make a significant contribution to the next stage of the change process. When faced with a decision of losing a spouse and family, many addicts are more willing to seek help and professional counseling. While their initial motivation for seeking help may be out of fear, it eventually transitions into a self-motivated desire for change. Real change comes about when clients shift from fear into self-motivation. This transition occurs over time as awareness, knowledge, and successful relapse prevention strategies are internalized.

DUTY

Duty contributes to the change process primarily because individuals sense or feel an obligation to the people around them. Many individuals have told me that they want to give up their addiction because of someone else. They feel that they have an obligation to their spouse, child, or employer. Most clients have told me that the key contributor to them coming to therapy was the responsibility they felt to take care of someone close to them. Here is a list of reasons given for change out of duty:

- Commitment to provide for family
- Obligation to an employer
- Responsibility to take care of child
- Religious duties or responsibilities

Generally speaking, a sense of duty helps create change when individuals begin to mature. As young adults become more mature and have more responsibility they often change out of obligation. We hear statements such as, "I realized that I had to stop fooling around and get serious when I met the girl of my dreams." For many addicts this maturity level comes with time and added society or family responsibilities.

To illustrate this point, consider a national survey assessing drug or alcohol abuse or dependence. The researchers found that 18–25 years olds make up 22 percent of all abusing or dependant individuals. By comparison, 40–44 year olds make up for 9 percent of dependent or abusing addicts. Similar findings have been found with virtually every other illicit drug. According to national experts, even the number of cigarette smokers goes down rapidly after age 19. Researchers have found that "among all racial/ethnic groups, smoking initiation occurred approximately at age 9, increased rapidly with successive ages after age 11, peaked at 17 to 19, and declined substantially after age 19."[2] Clearly, the age group that we see the most addictive behaviors is between the ages of 18 and 25. Based on these findings, the majority of these young adults will mature and their addictive behaviors will decrease after the age of 25.

It could be argued that having a spouse, child, job, and other duties significantly impacts this population as they find their role in life and begin taking more responsibility, which in turn creates less time for addictive activities. Many addicts choose to live more mature lives when they have a reason to. Clients often disclose to me that they want to quit viewing pornography because they don't want to let down their wife or girlfriend. Others say, "I don't want my children to think that this is appropriate behavior." When duty and responsibility are the reasons given for change, there is often a relationship that drives the desire to change. It is in relationships that most people find added responsibility and a reason to change.

Another common reason for quitting addictive behaviors is the interference it creates with work responsibilities and duties. One client put it this way, "I am so busy with my job that if I was involved in pornography, I wouldn't be able to keep up with my demanding schedule. My job will always take precedence over pornography." The fear of losing a job or being unable to perform tasks while at work adds reason for the pornography addicted person to quit or monitor his behaviors, such as staying up late viewing pornography.

LOVE

Inside most of us there is a desire to find love. When love is noticeably absent from an individual's life the loneliness is often soothed over by behaviors that hide or mask the internal emptiness. Often the life story of addicts is one of hurt and pain in their family relationships. The following story is representative of many of the clients with whom I have worked over the years.

Johnny came from a home where his father committed suicide when he was ten years old. Prior to his father's death he saw his dad repeatedly abuse his mother and then turn to the children and threaten him and his siblings. By the age of ten he found how to rub himself sexually when he was stressed. Not fully understanding the feelings, he continued this behavior each time he was in high stress. He married at a young age after getting his wife pregnant. Over time his relationship with her was not enough. His sexual misbehaviors extended to many areas (voyeurism, pornography, and visiting novelty stores). When his wife discovered his behavior he finally had to stop and evaluate his actions. In his entire life he had never really connected with another person. Even his sexual relationship with his wife was just a "rush." As he sought help he finally learned that he had had many limited relationships over the years but he had never formed a really close bond or loving relationship with anyone. He found that what he was really looking for was a true and loving relationship. For the first time in his life he began developing close relationships with others, and eventually he was able to develop a deep connection with his wife.

In many cases like Johnny's, the addictive behavior develops when the individual feels alone, isolated, or overly stressed. However, when this same individual does find a relationship, it fills the sexual void and the desire for the addictive behavior often dissipates while the relationship fills the void. However, without the proper tools in place when the need for a sexual high comes back or the relationship is no longer filling the void, the human mind will quickly resort back to the previously used solution to cope with any negative internal feelings.

What is missing from the lives of many pornography addicted clients is a healthy relationship. Notice the word healthy. When relationships are not going well or there is no intimacy, it is easy to turn to an unhealthy and potentially addictive behavior for comfort. Feelings of isolation and loneliness are common emotions for unmarried and married individuals. On the other hand, a positive loving relationship has the ability to soothe the desire to find quick or instant gratification.

Author Victor L. Brown has said, "The lives of most people are histories of their search for intimacy, of their attempts to be socially, physically, and emotionally close to others."[3] Inside most of us is the drive for acceptance, love, and intimacy. When we have intimacy with others the need for outside gratification is reduced. However, without a connection to others there is a void that has to be filled with something. When this void is filled with pornography, the long-term challenge is learning how to give up this addictive behavior when it is so readily available. Furthermore, many who struggle with pornography or a sexual addiction have never experienced a close and intimate relationship.

Love on the other hand is very powerful and can be used as a change agent. One man shared the following story with me. He said one night he was out drinking with his buddies when he bumped into his girlfriend. She said to him, "either or," meaning either me or the drinking. He told me that was the last time he ever drank. Now, fifty years later, he said that was the wake up call that he needed. His love for her helped him stop drinking. While love is not always so powerful, it truly can be a constant reminder to make the addicted want to be better.

I have met others who have attempted to quit pornography because they are in love. While love can lead to a temporary reduction in the desire to look at pornography, it seldom lasts without obtaining additional tools and resources to maintain the change. Some individuals mistakenly believe that because they are in a loving relationship they will never have problems again. Unfortunately, they have overlooked their history with pornography and downplayed the level of challenge they will face.

Such was the case with Tom. He came into my office having seen pornography every day for weeks. He had wireless Internet on his phone and reported viewing pornography on his phone various times each day. When he told me that he was sure he was done looking at pornography because he had a girlfriend, I looked at him and told him outright that I didn't believe he could make it more than two weeks without looking at pornography. I further told him that he would need extensive help to quit his addiction, but he didn't believe me. When he in fact did not last two weeks, he became more attentive in our sessions. As our relationship progressed he realized that his love for his girlfriend didn't offset the power of his addiction. He struggled mightily to overcome the quick fix he received when viewing pornography.

While love can be a motivational factor for change to occur it cannot be the only reason given for change. There needs to be an internal drive and desire to change. Once this occurs, love for self and others can be a great asset for overcoming a pornography addiction.

Fear, duty, or love can motivate a person to change from the contemplation stage to the preparation stage. However, without gaining personal insight into the addiction and how it can be overcome, relapse is almost inevitable. That is why it is critical to move from the contemplation stage to the preparation stage. One reason for staying at the contemplation stage is that many people simply do not know the steps to take to ask the necessary questions. They say to themselves, "I want to change—now what?" The preparation stage (discussed in the next chapter) helps individuals gain insight and awareness into how they can change. The preparation stage is a critical time period for those who genuinely want to change their lives and overcome their addiction. In the book of Hosea in the Bible it reads, "My people are destroyed for a lack of knowledge. . . ." Preparation is a key step to creating change.

Exercise 35: *What would be most likely to motivate you to change: fear, duty, or love? Please explain your answer.*

Chapter 6:
Preparing to Change for Good

"As we learn we always change, and so our perception. This changed perception then becomes a new Teacher inside each of us."

—*Hyemeyohsts Storm*

Often clients say, "I want to change, I really do, but I don't know where to turn or what to do. I have tried everything I can think of." When such feelings of hopelessness and helplessness enter the human mind it requires something positive to happen for hope to return. Far too often individuals stuck in the rut of pornography get an overwhelmed feeling that they cannot change. Fortunately, change comes when new ideas and answers are carefully considered. In learning new ideas and seeking answers, new strategies are practiced until they create the necessary hope to create lasting change. However, changing for good requires sufficient preparation or old habits and patterns are likely to return.

When I was a college student I worked summers building foundations for new homes. I was always surprised at the accuracy of my coworkers. They had spent years developing and honing their construction skills. However, in the first few weeks I couldn't understand why they would spend so much time looking at and evaluating the house floor plans. Before we did anything they checked over the plans and identified the exact dimensions of the home over and over again. I didn't fully understand this until they told me that if they were off by even an inch the framers and others could have problems. While working construction I learned many valuable lessons, but the most helpful was the importance of planning and preparation.

Preparation and planning are vital in overcoming a pornography addiction. So you may be asking, "What are the things I need to prepare?" Some of the important preparation elements have already been discussed such as understanding how the addiction developed and, in particular, the reaction sequence. In this chapter the focus will be key elements of preparation. They include:

- Defining sobriety
- Defining your boundaries
- Establishing goals
- Identifying your support team
- Forecasting and performing fire drills to help fight the pending battles
- Learning what to do when you don't know what to do
- Challenging questions

PREPARATION

DEFINING SOBRIETY

During the preparation stage it is important to clearly define sobriety. Without a clear definition it is easy to ignore behaviors that lead to relapse. For example, when Tyson decided to stop looking at pornography he concluded that online pornography was his biggest problem, so he resolved to stop looking at pornography online. With this definition he tried as hard as he could to fend off the craving to view online pornography. However, when television shows or movies showed nudity, he wasn't prepared for the challenge they would create. Initially he ignored the fact that he was viewing pornography (just in a different way). Then when he started back into online pornography he realized that his relapse was directly attributable to viewing pornography via television shows or movies.

His next step was more difficult. He had learned to avoid online pornography and had limited his television and movies to specific shows and movie ratings. He had succeeded in not viewing pornography for over six weeks, even when his cravings became intense. He struggled for the next few days with heavy withdrawal symptoms. After an in-depth discussion he realized he had been fantasizing about pornographic images during the past few days. With this realization he defined his sobriety as stopping fantasies a quickly as he could. His definition of sobriety changed with time and through learning experiences.

One commonly misunderstood element with a sexual addiction is that sobriety means not engaging in sexual behavior. This is not accurate. We are sexual beings and it is very natural to have sexual feelings and needs. The key element of sobriety is to define what it means to you and how it will impact your behaviors.

DEFINING YOUR BOUNDARIES

In preparing to succeed in overcoming a pornography addiction it is critical to define the rules or boundaries of what behaviors will prevent relapse. Defining these rules and boundaries takes time and energy. One question that often helps in identifying these boundaries is "What are the things that you simply cannot do if you are going to avoid relapse?" When answered honestly, this question can provide specific guidelines to help avoid relapse.

Isaac used this question to establish rules and boundaries. Initially his rules were very simple:

    a. Don't get online without someone being home.

    b. Don't watch TV alone after 11:00 P.M.

    c. When online, only visit specific sites.

    d. Don't drive down the streets that I know have pornography stores.

Over time and with experience, his outline grew. After he learned to track his emotions he included additional rules:

    e. When I am bored I will contact a friend or family member (these friends are Kyle, Mike, or Susan—family members include my wife and parents).

    f. If I am tired I will take a nap or if it is late at night I will go to sleep. If the thoughts or cravings don't go away I will sit down and write in my journal.

g. If I am stressed I will identify the reason and attempt to solve the problem rather than turn to pornography or another misbehavior. I will solve the problem by identifying it and looking for as many solutions as I can.

h. I will talk with someone when I have strong cravings or withdrawal symptoms.

With these rules and guidelines in place, Isaac found that he was succeeding most of the time. During the next few months he identified other triggers and implemented new rules or guidelines so he could succeed. He also learned that when he ignored his rules he would relapse. When he relapsed he identified the rule that he had broken and developed a new behavior to ensure that he would not break that rule again.

ESTABLISHING GOALS

During the preparation stage establishing goals can be very helpful. A goal gives individuals something to work toward and provides an additional purpose for fighting the battle. Even more importantly, a goal can help replace sexual thoughts and create additional desires to achieve higher thoughts. When in pursuit of positive thoughts the mind and body often become more energized and there is more purpose behind behaviors.

When a person becomes goal oriented his goals often drive him toward more focused and directed behaviors. Often, recovering addicts will turn toward more healthy behaviors. One man said he found preparing for a marathon was incredibly exciting and helped reduce his cravings. This is common, as researchers have suggested that addiction and excellence utilize the same patterns in the brain. Thus, achieving excellence in activities (running, art, music, etc.) may well be one of the most beneficial things a person can do to overcome a pornography addiction.

Obviously, not all people are goal oriented. However, those who do use goals can find great success in creating and carrying out their goals. For those who do not like goals it may be time to overcome such concerns.

Often people do not like goals because they feel like they will fail and they are afraid of failure (so it is better to not try than to try and fail). However, true failure comes when we do not try or stop trying. If you are not a goal-oriented person, learning to use goals can help you in the recovery process. This section will focus on how goals can help in the preparation stage.

Most people do not reach their goals because their goals are not developed or specific enough. It is common to hear goals like, "I want to quit looking at pornography." While this is the long-term goal it does not provide specific methods or ways that can be monitored and measured. A good goal is one that can be measured and evaluated on a regular basis. It should also include new positive behaviors that will replace old, negative behaviors. Here is a list of short-term, mid-range, and long-term goals.

Short-term goals:

1. *I will fight this battle one day at a time. I will measure this by:*
   Marking my progress on a calendar—if I succeed I will leave that day alone on the calendar. If I relapse I will place a mark on that day of the calendar. I will look for patterns of relapse.
2. *I need to spend less time fantasizing. Right now I don't know how much time I actually fantasize each day, so I will learn how much I am fantasizing using the follow strategy.*
   I will focus on reducing the time I spend thinking or fantasizing about sexual thoughts by measuring how much I am fantasizing each day. I will write down the time I spend fantasizing each day in a journal. The specific measure I will use is based upon a scale of one to ten (a score of ten means I have been fantasizing a lot during the day). I will track this for one month.
3. *I generally relapse when I am using the Internet so I am going to only use the computer when I have a purpose.*

In order to accomplish this goal for the next month I will only use the Internet to look at my email messages and visit sites that have a purpose (i.e., online banking and news sites).

4. I need more help than just my spouse or family. I will identify two more resources or people to help me.

I will find a counselor or group to attend to help me learn new ways to overcome this addiction. I will find a counselor or group in the next ten days. I will also identify two books to read on overcoming pornography addiction.

5. I will learn more about my patterns by understanding my reaction sequences.

I will write down my reaction sequence and I will review it at the end of each day for the next month.

6. I will identify my most common stresses that lead to viewing pornography and try to reduce them.

My finances have contributed to my stress level so I am going to develop a plan to reduce my debt. I will focus on reducing my debt by working longer hours two days a week. This money will be used to reduce my debt.

I also experience high stress when I am at work. I am going to look for a new job over the next few weeks. I will not quit this present job until I find a good job with which I am comfortable.

Mid-range goals:

1. I want to learn as much as I can about relapse prevention.

I will read about relapse prevention strategies and then identify my own relapse patterns. If I relapse I am going to write down what I could have done differently and identify the point I started planning my relapse.

2. I want to identify my relapse patterns (e.g., every two weeks) and go longer than I have in the past with no pornography.

If I find that I am relapsing about every two weeks I am going to set a goal to go as long as I can past two weeks without a relapse. Specifically, I want thirty days of sobriety and then I will work towards sixty days of sobriety.

3. I want to become an expert on understanding my withdrawal symptoms.

When I feel a withdrawal symptom I will have a pad of paper and pen to write down what I am experiencing. My purpose is to increase my awareness of the withdrawals I experience.

4. Learn about and engage in new relationships with the purpose of avoiding social isolation.

I want to develop three new relationships in the next two to three months. I want to replace my feelings of emptiness and isolation with new friendships. I am going to read a book on strengthening relationships.

5. I want to begin an exercise program that will help me prepare to run in 5K and 10K runs.

I will begin training three days a week to run in two 5K events and one 10K event. I will train for the next eight weeks in preparation for these events. I will run on Tuesday, Thursday, and Saturday mornings.

These mid-range goals will be evaluated over the next two to three months. During the next three months I will focus on these five areas so I can overcome this addiction.

Long-term goals:

1. Remain porn free for 180 days.

Building on my short-term and long-term goals I will avoid viewing pornography in any form for 180 days. In particular, I will not view Internet pornography or movies that have nudity. I will remain clean.

2. *I want to help others who are struggling with a pornography addiction.*

   I will do this by attending groups and sharing my experience with others.

3. *I will develop a healthy intimate relationship with my spouse/ fiancé or someone I date.*

   I will need to learn more about how to focus on relationships and spend time thinking about how successful relationships develop.

   I will need to improve my empathy and understanding of other's feelings. I will do this by asking more questions of the people I am with and trying to understand their perspective.

4. *I want to develop a new skill or hobby.*

   I am going to learn to play the guitar. When I am bored or think about relapsing I am going to pull out my guitar and practice. I will practice three days a week for thirty minutes.

The process of developing goals and plans can turn the mind's attention to more positive and productive behaviors. Goals should remain simple and achievable. If you feel overwhelmed by the goals you set it is a good idea to focus on just one or two. This is especially important for individuals who struggle with day-to-day abstinence.

Exercise 36: *Develop at least two short-term, mid-range, and long-term goals. Be as specific as you can and review your goals often.*

IDENTIFYING YOUR SUPPORT TEAM

Once a person decides he wants to change, he makes an internal resolution to do things differently. This is often short lived if it is a commitment that he makes only to himself. It is a common experience for the addicted person to promise himself he will never look at pornography again. This resolve can be strengthened, however, by including others in the struggle. When an individual begins seeking outside help and assistance he is taking good, positive steps toward real, lasting change. Talking to another person is in essence admitting that there is a problem and that is a critical step in overcoming pornography addiction.

It is common for individuals to begin this process by talking with a religious leader, a close friend, or family member. Sharing their behavior and getting it out into the open relieves a lot of internal turmoil. The secret they have been keeping inside is no longer bottled up. For some the power of admitting their behavior provides such a relief that they don't have any problems for weeks or months. In owning their behavior, their desire to resort back to the addictive behavior can diminish significantly and in some individuals almost goes completely away. This is what we call the honeymoon phase.

At this point it is a common mistake to believe the problem is over. Unfortunately, the honeymoon period ends and the reality of having an addiction comes forward. Withdrawal symptoms rise to the forefront and stress returns. This is when relapse is common, which often sends the individual back into the thought process of "I cannot do this." This is when it is easy to go back to the precontemplation or contemplation stage.

In truth, the only thing that changed is that the problem was no longer a secret. New skills and personal awareness of how to overcome the hard and stressful times were not developed or learned. That is why it is important for everyone who struggles with pornography to understand that change is a process that takes time and energy. It requires learning about the addiction, knowing how it developed, gaining insight into self, and knowing how to effectively deal with stress and trials. It also requires learning new behaviors to replace old, negative behaviors.

FORECASTING AND PERFORMING FIRE DRILLS

One of the most common methods taught in the preparation stage is called "fire drills." An example of this planning was described by Dr. Victor Cline.

He has his clients practice fire drills until they know what to do when faced with a challenge. Often they will practice these drills with a therapist or someone close to them. The focus is developing a plan of action that will be implemented when relapse is most common. This concept is similar to forecasting the potential challenges ahead. Here is an example from a therapist and client dialogue.

Therapist: Under what circumstances are you most likely to view pornography?

Client: I generally view pornography late at night when everyone else is asleep. I am tired and am just aimlessly surfing the web.

Therapist: If you are going to look at pornography, is this the way it is most likely to occur? Could you give me a percentage?

Client: I would say that this is the scenario seventy-five percent of the time.

Therapist: So if we were to change this pattern do you think you would find more success in not viewing pornography? Or do you think you would find other times to view it?

Client: I think it would reduce how much I look at pornography. I think it would help a lot.

Therapist: Okay then, let's put you in that very same circumstance right now. When does the first idea of looking at pornography come into your mind?

Client: If I am honest with myself it starts when I am watching television. It often starts by seeing a commercial or something else that is sexual in nature.

Therapist: So would you say this is the stimulus that gets you started?

Client: Yes.

Therapist: Okay, what happens next?

Client: I get pretty excited thinking about viewing pornography so I go up to my room under the guise that I am going to check my email. If no one else is around or I think that I can find something without anyone knowing, I will quickly check my email and then start looking for something pornographic in nature.

Therapist: Do you generally go to the same site or do you randomly look for pornography?

Client: I go to Yahoo or Google and do a random name search. Both of these sites get me started. Once at these sites I am led to other pornographic sites.

Therapist: I want you to imagine that you are up watching television. Across the screen comes a sexual scene. The thought comes to you to go and find something pornographic on your computer. The feeling is extremely powerful and you start to feel a chemical rush because you haven't viewed pornography for two weeks. What will you do?

Client: Under this circumstance I must first recognize that I am being challenged. I need to admit to myself that I am feeling like viewing pornography. Next I need to either go and talk with someone else, which is part of my game plan, or I need to think through what the outcome would be if I give in and look at pornography.

Therapist: What would keep you from taking these steps?

Client: When I relapse it is because I don't think of these things until I am on my computer.

Therapist: So let's suppose that you ignore the early signs and find yourself on the computer with a strong craving to view pornography. You have just checked your email and now you catch yourself at Yahoo. What will you do?

Client: This is harder because I am already feeling the chemical rush. Under these circumstances I have realized that I have to turn off the computer. Next, I have agreed to call someone else because I cannot fight it alone when the chemicals are that strong inside of me. If I cannot call because it is too late, I am going to sit down and write in my journal about what I am feeling. I will write until I have come up with a solution other than viewing pornography.

Forecasting potential circumstances and situations can be very helpful in fighting the battle with pornography. Notice the importance of being thorough and having a detailed plan or scheme for the times the challenges are most difficult. Fire drills offer one way to prepare for the battles ahead. This strategy can be implemented with all of the scenarios in which a person finds himself tempted by pornography.

CHALLENGING QUESTIONS

The following questions are challenge questions. The purpose is to invite the reader to contemplate how the addiction developed and how it began. The hope is that in understanding the answers to these questions, a more clear understanding will emerge as to why pornography has become such a dominant part of your life and how it can be changed. Here are some of the key questions that help in the preparation stage of change:

- How did I get so involved in pornography?
- How did my family or friends contribute to my involvement with pornography?
- Why do I look at pornography? What does it do for me?
- What measures can I take to reduce my exposure to pornography?
- Do I need to put limits on how much time I spend on the computer or where I use it? If so, how will I do this and when?
- What do I need to be the most cautious?
- What exactly do I need to change to reduce my involvement with pornography (e.g., less TV late at night, no random web surfing, no Internet if no one is around)?

During the preparation stage, identifying the answers to these questions can be very helpful in the difficult times. Such awareness can assist in the development of new behaviors.

In addition to the areas listed above, here are additional elements that can help in the preparation stage. A more thorough discussion of these preparation tools is listed below. Each of the steps listed helps in the next step, the "Taking-Action" step, which includes:

- Increasing an understanding of self and family background (review chapter 1)
- An increased awareness of the challenges ahead (i.e., withdrawal symptoms—see exercises in chapter 1)
- How and why the addiction started and what pornography does for you now (review exercises in chapters 1 and 2)
- The development of a specific plan of action when fighting the battle to look at pornography (review chapter 3)
- Beliefs that you have that contribute to the addictive behavior (chapter 4)
- Relapse prevention journal (chapter 9)

Chapter 7:
Taking Action and Maintenance—
The Behaviors of Changing for Good

"It is a matter first of beginning—and then following through."
—*Richard L. Evans*

The transition from the preparation stage to the taking action stage is an exciting time for most people. For the first time in years they feel hope that they can change. With a good plan in place there is generally some enthusiasm to move forward and overcome the pornography addiction. During the transition from preparation to taking action there is often a period of time in which the internal battle to view pornography is reduced. This can be attributed to moving away from the addictive behavior and toward a solution. During this time behavior is modified and the results can be seen. Previous behavioral patterns begin to change and old habits such as staying up late or randomly surfing the Internet stop. These behavioral changes can be seen and are clear signs that change is taking place.

In addition to behavioral changes there are internal changes that can be felt. The level of personal awareness increases and emotions become more upbeat and positive, self-image and confidence begins to increase and what a person thinks about also changes. These internal feelings are not only felt inside, but others can sense them. One client put it this way, "My girlfriend told me that she could feel my countenance change. She knows when I am doing well." During this phase there is more happiness and inner peace.

In particular, during the taking-action stage a person's self-awareness increases and his emotions become more stable.

TAKING ACTION

AWARENESS

As individuals gain more awareness into their level of pornography addiction they realize that they can learn and develop new behaviors. This process requires a clear and honest evaluation of self. As an observer it is not difficult to pick out those who have this awareness and those who do not. Brian's story illustrates this point. He was in his first year of sobriety and had been attending groups and individual counseling. Here is a short section of his story.

> "When I realized that there was no way to get out of the trouble my addiction was creating I was scared. I was sure I would lose everything. I had been in denial for years. I didn't dare look back because change wasn't possible for me. I was turning out just like my dad. Not until I went to a group and started learning about addiction did I realize that there was hope for me. Only when my therapist asked me to write my sexual history, how my family influenced my addiction, and how my addiction developed did I realize that I was conditioned for sexual deviance. I gained so much by simply understanding how my family dynamics contributed to my addiction."

As Brian gained more awareness about how his addiction developed he began looking for more ways to be aware. Soon he was trying to identify the trigger points that led to relapse. He began thinking about the things that he had previously dismissed as "not a big deal." He was able to identify certain elements: TV, magazine racks, R-rated movies, aimlessly surfing the Internet, and allowing fantasies to run at will through his mind. With this awareness he began making a conscious effort to alter these behaviors. Over a few months he was more capable of taking precautions to prevent relapse.

With an awareness of the key trigger points, Brian was able to move on to identifying his own inner thoughts and how they could help overcome his addiction. He developed an internal game plan to help fight the battle against pornography. Here are the general steps of an internal awareness game plan:

Recognition—when the first thought comes into your mind to look at pornography it is critical to recognize this thought. Success in this area can lead to a quick response. If alone, it may be helpful to stop and say "that is a common thought that has led me to view pornography in the past." Such awareness should raise the internal red flags signifying the need for caution.

Identify the source—Once the trigger point has been identified, now it is important to gain insight into the source of the trigger point. Was it the TV, Internet, a beautiful woman seen during the day, or a fantasy? It is important to identify and acknowledge the source. If it is the TV, then getting away from the TV is a critical step to success. The principle here is that you cannot relapse if you aren't in the situation. In other words, if you aren't at the bar it is hard to find a drink. Don't fight the battle at the bar.

Look at the outcome—The next step is to determine the outcome. What is the outcome of giving in and ignoring the trigger point? What is the outcome if you avoid the situation and do not give in? I encourage clients to look at both possibilities. For example, the common response of someone who is going to give in is "I feel frustration, guilt, and feelings of hopelessness." I often add, "and a quick sexual release that will bring temporary relief." It is important to be completely honest with all of the outcomes. The most common outcome of not giving in is inner strength and confidence, more hope, excitement that change is possible, and unfortunately, withdrawal symptoms. It is important to look at both possibilities.

In paying the price to do this each time the thought comes to view pornography, the old established patterns of the mind can be broken and new pathways can be developed. Furthermore, those who use this awareness are more prone to see the outcome of giving in. Most of my clients tell me they don't think in advance what the outcomes of viewing pornography could be. In the moment, the natural internal cravings take precedence. However, using the steps listed above provides great awareness into how to fight the addiction. The next step of awareness is to carry out the game plan.

> *Carrying out the game plan*—In chapter three a game plan was developed to help stop the reaction sequence. With the awareness that comes from using the three steps listed above, carrying out the game plan is the final step of taking action to openly fight and win the battle.

Here is an example of how this whole process could work.

John was watching late night television when he suddenly felt the urge to find something pornographic. First, he recognized what he was feeling. As soon as the thought came to his mind he said to himself, "I am in danger." Second, he identified the source. The source was the television. He also realized that he was alone and would be so for another hour or so. Third, he looked at the outcome if he didn't change his circumstances. He thought, "If I give in I will need to start all over." However, he also recognized that the chemicals had been released into his system and that he was feeling a strong craving for a sexual release. This concern led him to think about the consequences of giving in. He would need to report his behavior to his wife and his therapist. This process helped him recognize that he needed to do something different, so he went to his desk and reviewed the game plan he had previously developed. He decided to shut off the TV and go for a walk. While on his walk he thought about what he had just experienced and decided to call his wife when he got home to let her know he was struggling.

Notice that each of the elements listed above happen in the mind. This internal awareness helps in fighting the battle against viewing pornography. Why? It is easy to slip back into old habits without thinking about them. It is common for relapse to occur because previously established habits, patterns, or trigger points are never examined or altered.

Exercise 37: *How does your level of awareness influence your ability to fight off a craving to view pornography?*

EMOTIONS

Another element that helps in the taking-action stage is a clear understanding of one's own emotions. It is common to relapse when feelings of sadness, hopelessness, loneliness, or other negative thoughts are running through the mind. This is why recognizing emotions is so critical. More often than not, relapse occurs because individuals turn to pornography rather than working through their emotional pain or frustration. However, individuals in the taking-action stage have learned that if they can identify their true emotions they can do something other than view pornography when they are feeling down.

Isaac was accustomed to turning to pornography when he felt alone. He had no prospects of a relationship and felt completely isolated from everyone. He was clearly depressed because of his involvement with pornography. He had developed a pattern of looking at pornography when he was alone on the weekends. After he learned about reaction sequences and how the mind works, he began identifying his emotional states when he relapsed. He found that feeling alone and isolated triggered the thought to look at pornography. With this awareness he soon found it much easier to acknowledge his emotions and try to resolve them rather than ignore them and hope that they go away. Soon he had developed productive ways to cope with these negative feelings.

The added benefit of dealing with emotions is that they get resolved. When unhealthy emotions are resolved and positive solutions are found, the mind becomes less tense and more relaxed. Learning to solve emotional turmoil is extremely valuable in preventing relapse.

Exercise 38: *Describe the emotions that are most common to you. How do these emotions impact or influence your desire to view pornography?*

SELF-IMAGE

During the taking-action stage a person's identity or self-image begins to change. Many addicts report that their self-image was severely damaged by their behaviors. Living a lie or having secrets creates a made-up world where only the addict lives. Living a double life requires a lot of work and deception. The consequence is often a low image of self. Conversely, those who are taking actions necessary to change have a greater sense of growth and knowledge. Their self-confidence increases. They love learning and identifying new ways to overcome their addiction. They enjoy education, which is facilitated by attending a twelve-step group or counseling.

When a person's self-worth increases it can often be visibly seen. The transition from self-loathing to self-confidence takes time and concerted effort. Many sex, drugs, or alcohol anonymous groups have pins, medallions, or other mementos to award individuals with 30, 60, 90, etc. days of sobriety. This type of reward or recognition can lift the confidence of individuals who may have never received positive feedback in their entire life. Since our self-worth can be seen by others, the rewards of social acceptance are by-products of taking action to overcome pornography addiction.

Exercise 39: *How has pornography impacted your self-image? How is your self-image changing as you gain new information and knowledge about how to stop viewing pornography?*

THOUGHTS

"As a man thinketh, so is he." The mind of an individual struggling with pornography is often filled with feelings of guilt, shame, frustration, sadness, and depression. Pornography begins to take over this person's mind. No longer does the addict find hobbies, sports, and other activities as enjoyable. Pornography can seize control of the mind to the point that it spends little time thinking about other things. That is why an addict is willing to miss a social or sporting event in order to view pornography.

Individuals who have developed a game plan and are taking active measures to change will begin focusing their thoughts on other aspects of their life. The single person begins exploring dating and relationships. The married person becomes more involved in family life. Literally all areas of life begin to change. One man said, "For the first time in years I am able to enjoy the simple things in life. I cannot believe the things I have started doing again. My children are seeing a dad they haven't ever seen. I look back in disgust on all of the things I have missed out on." The joy of reclaiming the mind is a pleasure to see.

One way to evaluate progress in overcoming a pornography addiction is to identify what a person thinks about. Clearly, the less time a person fantasizes the better his chances of making sustained progress. One way to measure growth is by tracking whether a person is in fact spending less time fantasizing. In the taking-action stage there should be a significant reduction in the amount of fantasy that occurs in relation to how much fantasy was occurring at the precontemplation or contemplation stages.

FANTASIZING

Precontemplation—In this stage there is frequent fantasizing that can occupy hours of time each day. The fantasies are very explicit in nature and generally lead to some form of acting out (e.g., masturbation, finding and viewing pornography, acting out with someone).

Contemplation—Fantasy is frequent and is similar to the precontemplation stage. If the fantasies are recognized as a problem there may be attempts to stop or reduce them. However, more often than not most people define sobriety as not viewing pornography and do not consider how fantasizing can lead to viewing pornography.

Preparation—During the preparation stage fantasy is recognized as a trigger to relapse. Consequently, strategies are developed to try and stop the fantasizing. Common strategies such as the "STOP" method are implemented. The STOP method involves recognizing the fantasy and trying to get it out of the mind within three seconds. It also includes replacing the fantasy with a thought that is positive and productive.

Taking Action—In the taking-action stage fantasy is recognized as a key factor in relapse. Consequently, fantasy-type thoughts are quickly replaced. In addition, thoughts turn towards new goals and desired achievements. More time is spent thinking about work or school. During this phase time that used to be spent thinking about or viewing pornography turns toward other pursuits. More empathy and compassion are shown toward others. Spirituality and self-reliance increase and friendships and relationships are more authentic.

A key element of growth and development is regular evaluation and assessment. There are many behaviors and thoughts that have to be identified and changed during the taking-action stage. Here are a few exercises that can help in this process.

Exercise 40: *As you progress into the taking action stage what will you think about rather than pornography or fantasy?*

Exercise 41: *What will you do to stop the fantasies from running in your mind? Write down at least three things you can do to stop fantasizing.*

Exercise 42: *What actions are you currently taking to stop looking at pornography? How effective are these actions?*

Exercise 43: *What actions have you found to be most effective in helping you to stop viewing pornography?*

Exercise 44: *What actions do you need to do less of if you are going to completely stop viewing pornography?*

Exercise 45: *Review the last time you relapsed and identify specific actions that you could have taken to avoid the relapse.*

MAINTENANCE

In the book *Good to Great,* Jim Collins describes what makes the difference between companies that are good and companies that are great.[1] Ironically, most of the companies that excel were not fancy or glittering in any way. They were simple companies with a clear vision: they were consistent, reliable, and held to a consistent implementation plan. Individuals who are succeeding at overcoming pornography are much like these companies in that they demonstrate the qualities that help them succeed. A quote that demonstrates the plight of this stage comes from Willie Mays. He said, "It isn't hard to be good from time to time. . . . What's tough is being good every day."

When individuals consistently utilize the skills developed in the preparation stage they shift into the taking-action stage. Over time they develop more confidence in themselves and the tools they have learned. At this point they move into the maintenance stage. Emotionally they feel more calm and comfortable. For the first time in a long time they can step back and look at their life without feeling extreme guilt and shame. They see the progress they have made.

The successful person has learned that during the maintenance stage old behaviors are less desirous. Not because the craving has gone completely away, but because the alternative is too painful. Once a person has paid the price of overcoming the withdrawals, white-knuckling it through the tough times, he has a firm resolve to stay strong. One client described it this way, "I decided to stop in the middle of an episode. It really was my last time acting out. The cravings are still there but I wouldn't go back for anything. It was ruining my life. I hated the way it made me feel."

The person in the maintenance stage has come to realize that his personal growth and development has not come by chance; it requires a lot of work and effort. It demands that he never quit or let down his guard. An analogy could be made with running a marathon. The initial training is very difficult—motivation is low because the muscles become tight and the training feels like work. It would be much easier to stay in bed in the morning rather than get up at 6:00 A.M. to run. However, after a couple of weeks of training the muscles are more prepared and do not become sore. The body adjusts to getting up because new habits are being developed. Soon the runner begins to feel more energy and can lengthen the distance of the run. What initially seemed like a long distance is now a simple run. After consistent training and building up endurance the runner is prepared to run the marathon. As all marathon runners know, they will likely hit the wall. However, as they fight through that wall and keep going they realize they can and will reach their goal. Once the runner completes the race he can look back at his former self and realize that a significant change has occurred in his body and attitude.

Maintaining sobriety is much like preparing for and running a marathon—it requires a lot of work. The initial phases are very hard. They require strict discipline and grueling days. Eventually, enough preparation has been made and the race begins. In the initial stages there is strong motivation. However, the wall is eventually hit and withdrawal symptoms manifest themselves. Those who maintain sobriety realize all of their preparation has paid off and that quitting is not an option. As they make it through the withdrawals, the battle becomes less intense and the finish line becomes a legitimate possibility. While the real race for sobriety never stops, those who maintain it feel a genuine sense of accomplishment and have true inner peace.

It is important to note that during the maintenance stage relapse is less likely than at earlier stages. However, it is still a possibility and requires careful watch. One client said, "I had been doing well for over eight months and thought I had licked this problem. Then one day out of the blue I was in a familiar environment and was feeling a little down and depressed. Suddenly, within just seconds I found myself looking at something I didn't want to look at. Without going to my emergency game plan, I spent more time viewing pornography than I wanted to." As this client found out, letting down one's guard or relaxing previously erected barriers can quickly lead back to relapse. If an individual relapses in the maintenance stage, his response is critical. He can learn from his experience by identifying the triggers, learning the specific reasons why he relapsed, creating a plan to fight the battle better next time, or he can shame and guilt himself back to earlier stages and return to higher levels of pornography addiction.

The challenge with relapsing during the maintenance stage is to catch it quickly before old patterns and strong sexual feelings return. Generally speaking, individuals in the maintenance stage have been away from pornography for six months to two years. Consequently, a relapse can either be a blip on the radar or a hurricane waiting to happen. The final stage of changing for good, "relapse prevention," will be the focus of the next two chapters.

Chapter 8:
The Profile of Those Most Likely To Relapse

"Relapse is not an unfortunate event that happens to you; it is a series of bad choices that you make"
—Dr. Stanton Peele

While talking with a retired police officer who also served as an undercover drug agent I inquired about the profile of drug addicts. He identified many of the signs he looked for in drug addicts and then said that after years of doing undercover work he could point one out by simply watching them for a short period of time. As I pondered his confidence I began reviewing some of the more difficult cases I had dealt with over the years. I began taking mental notes and comparing clients who were successful and those who were most likely to relapse back into pornography. The following is the outcome of that exercise. Each characteristic of the profile will identify behaviors of individuals who are most prone to relapse and will offer solutions to combat these behaviors.

THE PROFILE OF THOSE WHO ARE MOST VULNERABLE TO RELAPSE

A profile is an analysis that represents a person or a process. The profile of those who are most prone to relapse has been developed by observation of clients who relapse and through listening to stories of clients who succeed. Interestingly, the story of successful clients is very consistent. They begin talking the same way as other clients who succeed and their behaviors change in similar ways. At the opposite end of the spectrum, clients who relapse demonstrate similar behaviors and use common justifications that lead to relapse.

The characteristics of those who are most likely to relapse are listed below.

- Keeping secrets
- Limited relationship connections
- Chronic conflict: arguing and fighting
- Little to no social interaction—isolation
- Living for intense and extreme experiences
- Leaving treatment prematurely
- Inadequate preparation
- Ignoring emotional issues

KEEPING SECRETS

Harry came to therapy because his religious leader had asked him to seek help before he was married. He had been dating Jennifer for many months and they had been discussing marriage. Harry was hesitant to get engaged because he realized that pornography was a problem for him. He had not discussed his involvement in pornography with Jennifer and was concerned how she might respond. As their relationship became more serious his involvement with pornography had gone from viewing three to five times a week to every few weeks.

Even with the encouragement of his leader he had put off calling me until his clergyman insisted that he do so. In our first session it was clear that Harry was concerned about his viewing pornography, but his biggest concern was how Jennifer would respond if she found out. He did not want to tell her. His religious leader had told him he needed to but Harry did not want to ruin his relationship. He worried that if she knew she would dump him and that he would get heavily involved with pornography again.

When I reinforced the need to discuss this with his girlfriend he became frustrated. He was sure that she would end the relationship. As we discussed how she would respond he began to realize that he was hurting her and would quickly destroy any trust she could have in him if he continued to ignore the real reason he wasn't pursuing an engagement. He decided to discuss his problem with her and realized that if he lost her it would be because he was being honest. This was a great start in our therapy work together.

Over the next few months we worked through all of the stages and included his girlfriend in the preparation and maintenance stages. She turned out to be a great resource for him as she was willing to talk with him when he was feeling most vulnerable to relapse. While some of my cases do not turn out this well, I am convinced that secrets destroy relationships. My policy is "No more secrets."

Those who keep secrets related to pornography often develop the following habits in life.

Lying—Lying becomes a necessity since it is virtually impossible to view pornography and not lie. The other problem with lying is that it takes a tremendous amount of time to cover up old lies. In the book *The Millionaire Mind* the author tells a story of an owner of a successful real estate management firm. The owner told his son, "Never lie. Never tell one lie. If you tell one lie, you will have to eventually tell fifteen more to cover up the first lie." Some of the common lies associated with pornography include:

- Telling one's spouse of the importance of staying up late to work on a project with the clear intent of viewing pornography
- Staying at work late under the guise of meeting a deadline
- Hiding and stashing magazines, pictures, downloaded video clips, and DVDs
- Creating reasons to not attend activities or events so that one can view pornography
- Minimizing the level of involvement in pornography
- Claiming innocence when pornography is found on your computer
- Not being honest with oneself, which includes ignoring internal feelings of guilt or shame. This is lying to oneself by avoiding the feelings and trying to cover them up
- When asked about involvement with pornography the answer is an attempt to deflect the question without a direct answer, or it is a flat out lie

Emotional inconsistency—Secrets create inner turmoil and strife, which creates a pattern of emotional ups and downs. Many addicts say that when they are doing things in secret they find they feel a tremendous amount of guilt and shame, which in turn triggers other negative feelings about self.

Internal mind games—The mind can create a lot of internal tension when secrets are held in. One client described it this way, "I view pornography then I spend hours trying to cover up my tracks. I wonder if my wife will find what I have seen or if I am at work I wonder if my boss knows what I am doing. At times I become so paranoid that I wonder if other people know that I have a problem with pornography." The only way to end these mind games is to begin telling the truth about the problem. Many addicts feel so strongly that others will reject them or criticize them that they believe it is better to keep their secret to themselves. The consequence is that they put themselves into a little isolation box where they feel like no one understands them. A common thought while in this box is, "If people only knew what I was really like they would not like me."

Low self-worth—Secrets often create feelings of low self-worth. It is very hard to feel good about oneself while hiding behaviors from others. It is common for individuals who create secrets to feel guilty and ashamed knowing that they are living a double life. As a result, many who are struggling with low self-worth often choose to numb the emotional pain that comes from these feelings with pornography. Consequently, a vicious cycle occurs between feeling low self-worth and then numbing that feeling away by viewing pornography. Then because all of this is a secret, those negative internal feelings about self lead to an increased chance of relapse.

Solutions for avoiding secrets

The solution for avoiding secrets is to have an accountability partner. This is a person who will regularly keep in contact with you. It is extremely helpful to tell him or her all of your struggles. It is also beneficial to share the goals that you have set so that you are accountable to someone.

This strategy was described by Dr. Stanton Peele in his book *7 Tools to Beat Addiction*.[1] He suggests you set up your own support system. This could be a spouse, friend, family member, or someone else who is concerned about your progress. In your first meeting you need to discuss the steps you each plan to take and schedule a fixed date within the next few weeks (no longer than one month). At that meeting, come prepared to discuss your behavior and its consequences—for example, review whether you accomplished your goals or not, evaluate your progress, and determine new goals for the next month. Whether you are successful or not in your attempt, review the actions you have taken and identify which steps you took that helped the most. At the end of your discussion, schedule a fixed date to meet again.

This strategy should be used to help you maintain accountability. As you decide who you would like to be an accountability partner, remember that this needs to be a person with whom you can be completely open and honest.

LIMITED RELATIONSHIP CONNECTIONS

Researchers have consistently found that individuals who do not have close relationship connections are more likely to engage in dangerous or harmful behaviors. One example of this can be found in the book *The Case for Marriage*.[2] In this book the authors report that single people are more likely to take risks and engage in behaviors that are unhealthy (e.g., not eating well, drinking, reckless driving, etc.) while married people engage in more healthy behaviors. While we do not have enough research to determine if married people view pornography more or less than singles, it would be fair to say that married people, in general, are less likely to engage in activities that are unhealthy and could put their relationship in danger.

Marriage, however, is not the only place a connection can occur. When individuals have close friendships and relationships with coworkers, church associates, a dating partner, or a family member, they are more likely to have a reason to fight their battle with pornography. When people have very few connections with others their feelings of being alone or that no one cares about them can quickly lead them back to relapse. One client put it this way, "When I was spending hours alone each day I did not see a purpose or reason for avoiding pornography." Individuals who are alone are much more prone to relapse than those who have supportive relationships.

Some relationships, however, make the battle with pornography even more difficult to fight. Many who are struggling with pornography also have trouble in relationships because they feel guilty and ashamed. In some instances they take their frustrations out on a spouse or partner, which creates further distance in the relationship. This leads to increased guilt and shame.

On the other hand, in a relationship in which there is a close connection and feeling of support, extra strength and desire to fight the battle occurs. In my experience, many partners are willing to try and help, but in more situations than not they do not know how to help. This is why counseling together and learning about pornography addiction together can be so helpful.

Those who are fortunate enough to have a partner who is willing to go through these challenges can learn to create a close relationship bond. In this type of relationship couples learn to share almost anything with their partner and they know that they will be understood. They are not afraid to share emotional ups and downs. In this type of relationship the addict has many reasons to fight and stay away from pornography.

Solutions for those with limited relationship connections

The key is to develop relationship connections where positive skills can be practiced. Some of the methods for doing this include:

- Create an inner confidence so you can succeed in relationships.
- Increase your empathy and compassion for others.
- Learn to deal with your negative emotions in positive ways.
- Develop positive communication skills.
- Learn good conflict resolution strategies.
- Learn to share emotions and challenges with a partner or friend.

CHRONIC CONFLICT: ARGUING AND FIGHTING

Charlie had been married for many years but he did not feel close to his wife. They argued about everything. Throughout the years he had developed a pattern of viewing pornography after big blow ups. Eventually she found pornography on his computer and confronted him with her finding. Initially he denied what she had found by lying that a friend had borrowed his computer and it was the friend who had viewed pornography. However, when she found pornography a second time on his computer she confronted him again. Her anger triggered a defensive response in him and he told her that he viewed pornography when they were arguing and fighting. His response is typical for many who find themselves in conflict situations.

When conflict is present in a marital, dating, working, or any other relationship, relapse is common. Most people do not like being in a conflict and as a result they turn to previously established places of comfort during these times. Unfortunately, most people do not know how to properly resolve conflict, which results in feelings of hopelessness and eventually relapse. Individuals who have had a problem with pornography and who are trying to stop viewing it will have a very difficult time avoiding relapse in an environment where there is regular conflict and where problems are seldom resolved.

Solutions for those accustomed to chronic conflict

If you are a person who is accustomed to conflict your challenge is to identify methods of resolving conflict. Life without conflict may be so counter to what you are used to that you may need to learn how to enjoy relationships. Here are some strategies for overcoming conflict in relationships:

- Rather than looking for the problems, learn to identify the positive aspects of your relationships.
- Before you get upset or angry at someone, step back and ask yourself how you could get your point across without hurting the other person.

- Try to look at all conflict from the other person's perspective before you respond.
- Avoid put-downs, criticism, and hurtful or negative comments about others, especially those to whom you are the closest.
- Send value to others in all of your communication.
- Develop relationships with people who are not negative and who look for the positive in others.

LITTLE TO NO SOCIAL INTERACTION

Austin had been fighting pornography for years and had been keeping his behavior a secret. The consequence was that he had isolated himself from everyone—he felt like no one would understand. He had heard people talk about the evils of pornography and he felt like he was too involved to let anyone know he had a problem. In isolating himself he found comfort in only one place, pornography. When Austin did make an attempt to be socially involved, they were very rarely good experiences. Each time he tried and it did not go well he became more frustrated. This led him deeper and deeper into his addiction and further and further away from others. When he tried to stop viewing pornography, the biggest obstacle was often the discouragement he felt from his lack of positive social interactions. He would justify a relapse by telling himself that nobody cared about him and that no woman would accept him.

Austin's story is a common one. Individuals who have limited social interaction are prime candidates for relapse. In many instances they feel shy and have fears that others will make fun of them. In social settings they worry so much about what others think about them that they cannot enjoy getting to know others. Often they leave early or try to get away. Far too often they do not have the social skills it takes to create positive social experiences. With a feeling of being inadequate and a lack of hope that they can change they turn back to pornography.

Solutions for little to no social interaction

In my practice I have had many single clients come to me struggling to identify how they can improve in their relationships. In an effort to help them I created an online test that I have called the Relationship IQ test. This 145-item test helps singles assess their dating and relationship skills and provides in-depth feedback and suggestions on how to improve in these areas. The results can help singles evaluate the areas where they can improve their social skills. This test can be found at www.growthclimate.com.

In Susan Page's book, *If I'm So Wonderful Why Am I Still Single?* she writes, "Wishful thinking has not brought you love. Neither has apathy, depression, denial, anger, panic, analyzing the problem, blaming the opposite sex, or cursing the bleak demographics."[3] As you seek a solution for little to no social interaction you need to get out and get involved with other people. It requires that you engage in activities that may make you uncomfortable. If you want social interaction you must find opportunities to meet people with whom you share common interests.

For some people this requires a whole new lifestyle. It means that beliefs telling you that there is something wrong with you must go out the window. Engaging in social activities may not be comfortable but when you have gained enough confidence you will see social activities as opportunities. In many of my cases I encourage clients to seek out social opportunities. This helps them focus on developing friendships rather than feeling sorry for themselves, and it also prevents them from focusing on their addiction. Here are some additional ideas for becoming more involved socially.

- Develop a list of activities with which you would like to be involved and do one or two each month. For example, Austin decided he would learn to dance.
- Set a goal to meet at least five new people a week.
- Attend at least one activity a week where you can meet people who have similar interests as yours.

- If you are single join a singles website and learn about others through online dating experiences.
- If you are married and looking for social interaction attend religious activities or invite neighbors over for a game night.

LIVING FOR INTENSE AND EXTREME EXPERIENCES

It is common for the pornography addict to have more than just one addiction. According to Dr. Carnes, 83 percent of sex addicts have other addictions.[4] One reason for multiple addictions is the need for intense experiences such as driving a fast car, rock climbing, hang gliding, or extremely physical workouts. Isolated, each of these behaviors appears normal, but for addicts they are necessary and provide a needed chemical high. In fact, many addicts simply cannot live without some form of regular intense experience. Some of the places people look for a high include:

- Spending money
- Using drugs
- Gambling
- Sex
- Overeating
- Exercise
- Spirituality
- Work

Those who have developed the need for constant highs often try to quit one addiction and while they are stopping one addiction they turn to another addictive behavior to get their high. Consequently, in assessing a pornography addiction it is important to determine if multiple addictions are present. This will help individuals recognize that pornography is just one of the addictions with which they are dealing, and unless dealt with holistically they are likely to return to pornography. In situations in which there are many addictions the goal should not just be treating pornography addiction, but teaching about multiple addictions and the ability to reduce the need for getting a constant high.

Solutions for those who need intense or extreme experiences

The first part of seeking a solution is identifying how many addictive or potentially addictive behaviors in which you are engaged. As you identify each of these issues it will be important to create strategies for fighting these battles. You can use the reaction sequence outlined in Appendix A to create a game plan.

The second idea for dealing with the need to obtain a high is to identify your personal reasons for needing the high. Most people have raised their tolerance level so high that when they are not getting some type of a high, they are frustrated or irritated. Without the high, fighting the withdrawal is very difficult. This is why it is important to learn how to lower the need for a high. It takes time to reduce the need for a high, but in the meantime, learning how to get a high from healthy behaviors is a good idea. Here is a list of alternative ways to get a high.

- Exercise (not excessive—no more than three hours a day)
- Spirituality
- Learning (e.g., attending college, reading educational books)
- Developing healthy relationships
- Learning a new skill, talent, or hobby
- Serving others

LEAVING TREATMENT PREMATURELY

Robert had a problem with pornography. However, when he came to therapy he was not seeking help because he wanted assistance. He was coming to satisfy others. In our first session he made it clear that we would come for two or three sessions. After our third session of therapy he declared that he was cured. Knowing his background and how involved he had been with pornography during his childhood, I recommended that if he was going to end therapy then he should build and maintain a support system for the next few months and perhaps the next couple of years. He told me that he was confident that he would not relapse. When I asked what he had learned in therapy he said, "I pretty much knew most of this stuff already, now I just have to do it." I was concerned that he was not fully prepared for the battles ahead, but he was confident. At that point he had not viewed pornography for four months. A few months later I received a phone a call from Robert; he had relapsed and this time was more interested in receiving help.

As is typical in situations like this, he had overzealously declared that he was done viewing pornography. In contrast, those who end up succeeding realize that periodically they may need to seek additional help. They leave the option open to return to counseling or groups at any time. Another mistake Robert made was that he refused to seek outside support. For those who leave treatment prematurely, if they have an outside support system there is still the possibility that they can succeed. Those who are most successful in their battle with pornography actually keep someone close to them. They have an accountability partner—someone with whom they can report their progress and struggles.

If you were asked the question, "How will you know you have overcome this addiction?" how would you respond? A response of those who are most likely to avoid relapse is, "I don't know if I will ever be able to say I have completely overcome this, but I know that if I stick to my plan I can succeed."

Solutions for leaving treatment prematurely

If you are a person who is inclined to quit treatment prematurely, the best thing you can do is make a commitment to continue learning. Relapse for sexual addiction is the most difficult during the six month to one year time frame. If you want to ensure that you are going to be successful this time, make a commitment that you are going to continue learning how to overcome your pornography addiction. Here are some suggestions that you can use to keep learning:

- Sign up for a newsletter (e.g., I have an e-zine called "Under-standing & Overcoming Pornography Addiction" that comes out once a month).
- Read a book about addictions and how to overcome them (see my recommended reading list in the back of this book).
- Attend groups consistently for the first year.
- Stay close to an accountability partner for 12 to 18 months. Report to your accountability partner at least once a month.
- Keep in touch with a counselor. Many of my clients have an agreement with me indicating that they can call me at any time if they need a tune-up. In these appointments we discuss challenges they have experienced and successes they are having. We also review any relapses and develop new strategies.

INADEQUATE PREPARATION

Preparation is very important for success in overcoming an addiction. The primary purpose for preparation is gaining new knowledge and tools to help in the fight. Far too often inadequate preparation is the reason for relapse. Often in my initial sessions with clients I ask them what they have done to attempt to quit viewing pornography. In many instances their attempts have been very limited. Few have ever read a book or gone to therapy. They simply did not know how to start or where to turn to get help.

Unfortunately, many people who do seek help quit before they have adequately prepared. When this occurs relapse is the likely outcome. The root of this problem stems from taking a little bit of knowledge and assuming that that information will be adequate for winning the battle. Then when relapse does occur it is easy to assume that counseling or therapy did not work.

Under most circumstances those who are fighting this battle with pornography need to be prepared to put extra time and energy into the fight. Overcoming pornography is not easy—it requires time and effort and it demands commitment. Over time those individuals who pay the price and adequately prepare reap the benefits of their efforts. Conversely, those who want the quick fix and an easy way out end up relapsing and develop an attitude that nothing works. Anyone who promises a quick fix for any addiction (pornography included) is overlooking the withdrawal symptoms and the simple access that our society has provided to addictive behaviors.

The process of developing a good plan is something that develops with time. It has been suggested that the preparation stage can take more than one year. Most of the clients with whom I work do not like to hear this, but real preparation does not happen in a day. Generally, success comes from learning about the addiction, preparing a game plan, carrying out the game plan, and reviewing what is working and what is not working. Learning from mistakes and gaining more information about how to fight against pornography is very important. This is why inadequate preparation so often leads to higher rates of relapse.

Solutions for inadequate preparation

Here are some questions you can ask yourself about your preparation to overcome your pornography addiction. This list could be used as a checklist in determining if one is prepared to win this battle.

- Have you learned how to break isolation?
- Can you survive withdrawal?
- Have you resolved or reduced any feelings of shame or guilt?
- Have you learned how to work through negative emotions?
- Do you know how to resolve crises without turning to misbehaviors?
- Have you adequately defined what sobriety is to you?
- Have you reviewed your reaction sequence and developed a solid game plan?
- Do you have an accountability partner?

IGNORING EMOTIONAL ISSUES

Our emotions are the internal indicators that tell us how we are doing. Sadly, when most people are experiencing these emotions they do not know how to resolve them so they turn to some form of misbehavior (e.g., pornography, abuse, substance abuse, reckless behavior, etc.). In our society we seldom teach people how to deal with feelings of sadness, loneliness, boredom, frustration, anger, or other negative emotions. As a result, most people turn to quick fixes because it is not fun to stay in a state of being emotionally frustrated. When emotions are not dealt with in appropriate ways relapse is the likely outcome. Some of the common emotions that lead to relapse include:

- Curiosity
- Need for excitement
- Frustration/stress
- Irritation
- Anger
- Boredom
- Pain
- Loneliness
- Worry
- Fear

Far too often people live in a state of emotional numbness. This comes from a lack of knowing how to resolve problems. When we do not know how to solve something our mind wants to take us to a place of safety, but when we are in this mindset we simply survive rather than thrive. Survival is the primary mechanism in all of us, which is why we flee into safety when we do not know how to solve problems. Safety is the place we go when the answers to our problems are not easily solved. For people dealing with pornography addiction, they are in safety when they allow feelings of hopelessness and helplessness guide their behaviors. At this point they give up on trying to overcome their addiction and say there is nothing they can do to win the battle.

Solutions for those who ignore emotional issues

A common practice is to ignore our emotions. Most people attempt to hide their emotions because they do not know what to do with them. The consequence is that they are buried. However, emotions buried alive never really die. They reemerge and wiggle their way back into our lives. As a therapist I often see individuals who have been hiding their true emotions from themselves and others because they are afraid of them. They stuff them inside. In a good treatment program emotions must be dealt with. Learning how to understand and deal with negative emotions is one of the most important techniques we can ever learn. I often tell my clients that if I could teach the world one thing it would be to deal appropriately with their emotions.

The process of becoming emotionally mature involves key steps of learning how to process emotions (ours and others). This begins by evaluating our own personal thoughts and feelings. It requires being completely open and honest with what you are feeling. This can be done by writing down personal thoughts and feelings, thinking through the emotions, or talking about them. For example, suppose the person you are dating told you that she didn't want to attend a party with you this weekend. In processing your emotions you would need to identify your initial thoughts and feelings (e.g., I was angry), then describe the emotion and its impact on you (e.g., my anger turned into ignoring you and blaming you for all of our problems).

The next step is to dig deeper into your anger. What was the underlying emotion behind the anger (e.g., I was hurt when you said you didn't want me to come to the party with you). The next step is to reevaluate how that emotion impacted your behaviors (e.g., I got upset and angry and refused to talk all night long). Next, identify what you would like to have done (e.g., I could have told you that I wanted to come with you and was hurt that you didn't feel like going with me). As you process your emotions you gain more control of your life because you are in control of your emotions.

Another part of emotional maturity is recognizing other's emotions. Emotional maturity means turning away from a preoccupation with your own needs and becoming aware of the needs of the people around you. Individuals who are stuck in an addiction often feel so self-aware and conscious of their own mistakes that they have a hard time meeting the emotional needs of others. While many people are aware of other's emotional needs, they do not know how to provide good and solid assistance. A common occurrence is to give too much advice rather than letting people talk through their problems and come up with good conclusions on their own. Those who learn to listen and be available to help others in emotional times have a talent that is invaluable.

Chapter 9:
Relapse Prevention Journal—A Tool to Use in Recovery

"Our own thoughts can set us free if we but learn to utilize them."
—Anonymous

This book offers many tools helpful to overcoming a pornography addiction. This chapter introduces a new technique: keeping a personal journal of your struggle. Through a sample journal we will see how this method can aid in recovery and provide valuable relapse prevention strategies. This journal will highlight some of the tools already discussed and illustrate how to use these tools in recovery.

RELAPSE PREVENTION JOURNALING: HOW WRITING AND TELLING YOUR STORY CAN HELP IN RECOVERY

The power of journaling is often overlooked as a healing method or tool that can be used in therapy. For those who have learned to use it, however, it has proven invaluable for finding the extra strength that is often necessary to successfully fight off addictions. Writing in a journal has also been found to be effective in reducing depression and other emotional problems.

Contrary to popular belief, writing in a journal is not simply writing the events of the day. It should be much more than that. A good journal can be used in identifying problems and learning new strategies to overcome life challenges. Each entry in this chapter's sample journal is used to emphasize the tools previously discussed in this book and how a person can journal throughout his recovery process.

The key elements a journal could include are listed below:

- It needs to offer a place where you can write down whatever you want to say. If you feel like you cannot be honest with what you are feeling, your journal will be limited in how it can help you.
- You should be as open and honest as you can about your feelings. If you are afraid to be completely open about yourself to others, a journal can help you learn how to express your deepest thoughts, feelings, and concerns.
- You should discuss your emotions (happy, sad, disgusted, frustrated, fearful, etc.)
- When writing, do not edit or be hesitant to write down any thought that comes into your mind. Just write! Let your mind be free and write down whatever thoughts come to you.
- When you have completed your daily entry, review what you have learned and write down these thoughts.
- As you look at your thoughts and emotions, start asking yourself questions that could lead to solutions. These questions should be written down as well. For example, how can I reduce my need to get a chemical high? The next step is to listen to whatever thought comes into your mind and write it down.
- Identify the behaviors you want to change as a result of your journal writing.
- As time moves forward, re-read previous entries to see how you are progressing and write down the achievements you have seen.

JOURNAL ENTRY: MAY 16, 2005

Dear Journal,

I have been asked to start writing my thoughts and feelings down in a journal. The truth is I am not much into journaling, but if it will help me overcome my pornography addiction I will do it. After meeting with my therapist I think he may have some ideas that will help. I felt more hope as I left his office than I have in a long time. I still cannot believe that I need to go to counseling because of this crap. I should be able to stop this on my own. Can I tell you how much I hate pornography? It makes me sick just to think about how I have let it take control of my life. Today was my first session with my counselor. He asked me to start writing down my thoughts about what I am learning in our sessions and he wants me to start writing my history of involvement with pornography.

In today's session I learned about what they call a reaction sequence. I couldn't believe how accurate he was in describing the build-up process, starting with the stimulus and ending with the behavior (me looking at pornography). He asked me to identify when I am most vulnerable to experience this reaction sequence. Here's what I've come up with:

When I am alone I often start thinking that I could look at pornography. This is especially true if I know that I am going to be alone for extended periods of time.

When I'm alone I feel like others don't care much about me. When I feel isolated or like no one cares I am especially vulnerable.

I also view pornography when I am stressed out. I think it is what I turn to under pressure. Sometimes I use it just to avoid things I don't want to do.

Anytime there is conflict in my life I turn to pornography.

Another time I view pornography is when I am bored. It isn't often that I am bored, but when I am the first thing that comes into my mind is to look at pornography. My therapist nailed it when he said that in certain circumstances I will almost automatically think about looking at pornography. When he described it like Pavlov's dog salivating when it heard the bell ring, it made sense to me. It is like my mind begins to salivate when I am bored.

As my therapist discussed how this reaction sequence develops I began realizing that I am so used to giving in and viewing pornography that I don't even think before I look anymore. When the stimulus first starts I quickly find a way to get to my computer and look at pornography. The therapist also explained to me that I have developed a need to get a chemical high. Chemicals! At first it made me think of drugs, which is never something

I've been into. But he made it make sense, and I was surprised at how many chemicals are released into my body when I view pornography. He asked me to identify the beliefs I have that "authorize" me (that's the word he used) to look at pornography. Here's the list:

- Pornography isn't that bad.
- Everyone else is doing it.
- I have been doing it for so long one more time won't hurt.
- I deserve it. This one is especially strong when I have had a bad day at work or my family relationships are not going well.
- Nobody will know and nobody really cares.
- It is just a form of entertainment.

It is interesting writing down those beliefs. I can see how they are warped, but it is hard to overcome them in the moment. There are two more things my therapist asked me to do. He wants me to write down my own reaction sequence and create a game plan for what I can do to rewrite a new one. This is going to be tricky, but here's what I've come up with so far:

Stimulus—There are so many things that get me thinking about looking at pornography. Watching late night television, randomly surfing the Internet, seeing a woman dressed in sexy clothes—even some of my music gets me thinking about pornography.

Emotion—I would say excitement and anticipation.

Thought—After the stimulus happens my first thought is to go and get on the computer. Or I sometimes will start thinking of ways I can be alone to view pornography.

Chemical Release—I am sure I get all of the chemicals the therapist talked about. He wants me to start recognizing when I think they are in my body.

Body Language—My body starts to feel a strong pull to view pornography. I can feel my heartbeat increase. My hands become cold and I can feel my head has more pressure on it. I also am likely to get an erection.

Thought—He called this the battle. I don't have much of a battle anymore since giving in has become such a part of me. However, there was a time when I would try and fight it. When I do fight the battle in my head it goes something like this:

Against-it thoughts:

I shouldn't be doing this. Why can't I just stop looking at this stuff? I need to stop some time.

For-it thoughts:

It is okay if you just look at a little. Just click on one site to see if you can see something. It wouldn't hurt to just look at women in swimsuits. I really deserve this. I need something to relax me. No one will find out.

Normally my "for-it thoughts" win. I wonder why?

Belief—My beliefs are listed above. I didn't realize how those thoughts really are my beliefs. They are the thoughts that I use to justify looking at pornography.

Behavior—When I accept those beliefs without question I end up finding pornography and masturbating.

I am amazed at how accurately this describes the process. Over the next few days I will think about this process and come up with a game plan for how to rewrite it.

Key points of what I learned today:

I learned about reaction sequences. It is pretty cool seeing how the whole process works. It makes sense to me now that someone has taken the time to carefully explain it to me. Now the challenge is learning to rewrite the reaction sequence so I can succeed. The really big news I learned today is that I am addicted to the chemicals. I realized I am addicted to the high I get when viewing pornography. In our session today my counselor discussed with me the need to lower the need for those chemicals. But he warned me that this would take time. I wish I could just get over all of it right now!

I am coming to realize that I am not alone—there really are other people who have this same problem. I didn't realize how much a part of my life pornography has become. I sure want to change; I hope this works. There is one other noteworthy thing. In therapy we discussed that I am in between the contemplation stage and the preparation stage. My therapist discussed the importance of me realizing that overcoming pornography is a process and that it takes time to develop the right knowledge and skills. That provides me some needed hope, which is something I haven't had much of in a long, long time.

Things I am going to work on:

I am going to review my reaction sequence each day this week (it's funny how this terminology is getting so familiar to me now). I have decided that I will develop a game plan over the next few days before I meet with my therapist again.

I want to teach my body that it doesn't need to keep getting a high from pornography. I am not sure how to do this yet, but I will think about it. We talked about how I may need to replace the need for that high with other activities. I am not sure what that is yet.

JOURNAL ENTRY: MAY 19, 2005

Dear Journal,

I was alone this morning and almost ended up relapsing. I was doing my typical pattern of looking at news websites and checking my email. Then I had the thought to go to a search engine and look for pornography. The thought was very powerful, but I quickly thought about what I had been learning about reaction sequences and realized a powerful chemical release was just around the corner. At that point, I pulled out the reaction sequence I created and reread it. I saw myself at the point that I could choose to allow more chemicals into my mind or I could do something else. Today I chose to do something else. I think I can learn from this experience. It taught me some new things. I have been thinking about how I can rewrite my reaction sequence with today's experience, and now I'm pretty sure I have devised a good plan.

My plan is pretty simple. I realized that I really need to get the thoughts out of my head as quickly as possible. This is not easy. Probably the biggest challenge is when I wake up in the morning and feel sexually aroused. In the past this is when I would get online, look up some news sites, and then view pornography until I had to be somewhere. I realized that if I am sexually aroused in the morning that I need to get up and get going or I am going to relapse. So here's my game plan for the mornings.

- Get up rather than linger in bed.
- Eat breakfast.
- Shower.
- If I have time to get online it will be with the specific purpose of just reading the news. If I find that the desire is strong to view pornography, I will have to avoid the Internet altogether and read a book instead. I will have a book that I can read at my side all of the time.

When my therapist asked me to write down a game plan I thought to myself, "How is this any different than just trying to stop the behavior?" However, I am realizing that if I write down a specific plan it makes it more real. My therapist also asked me to make a plan for each of the times I am most vulnerable. I will need to work on a game plan for late evenings.

Key points of what I learned today:

I realized that I am still very vulnerable to relapse. I was so close this morning and felt the chemicals creeping into my system. I learned today that I can stop them from entering by doing other things. If I am going to rewrite my reaction sequence I am going to need to pay close attention to the times when I am getting close to relapse and identify the things that work. Today I feel good about myself. I didn't relapse when I normally would have.

Things I am going to work on:

I have been reading my reaction sequence pattern and it helped me succeed today. Now I need to practice creating a new behavior. I decided that

I am going to focus on winning the morning battle by getting out of bed, eating, showering, and if the desire is strong, reading a good book.

I have been focusing on the chemical responses I feel when I think of sexual things. I have realized that my fantasies are contributing to the chemical release in my system. I really need to focus on thinking about other things than pornography and sex.

JOURNAL ENTRY: MAY 23, 2005

Dear Journal,

I met with my therapist again today. I shared with him my game plan and the journal entries I have had. His feedback was positive, but he also cautioned me about the upcoming challenges ahead. He asked me to identify how often I have been viewing pornography. I told him about every ten days to two weeks. He indicated that that pattern is one that we need to start breaking. Consequently, I am really going to work hard this week to focus my thoughts on being productive and focusing on the tasks I need to accomplish.

My therapist also cautioned me that the need for the chemicals might leave me with withdrawal symptoms. He asked me to identify any withdrawal symptoms I have experienced in the past when I have tried to stop. The biggest one is high sexual arousal. I get to the point where the craving and desire is so strong I feel like it is driving me to give in. He indicated that was a withdrawal symptom and that I needed to understand that I was experiencing the withdrawal in the moment it was happening. I will work on identifying the withdrawal symptoms.

Today my therapist also asked me to start looking at how my addiction developed. I am going to write down the circumstances that led me to view so much pornography while I was a teenager. The truth is, I have already thought some about this. I was home alone. I spent a lot of time by myself. I think my parents' fighting in the evenings didn't help. I realized that when they would fight I would turn to pornography because I didn't know how to deal with the yelling. I wanted to intervene and tell them to grow up. Instead

I turned to pornography. So I guess in answering the question the key parts that led me to pornography were:

- I was home alone almost every day. (My parents thought the filter on the computer would stop me from looking. Little did they know that I could find a way around it.)
- My parents' fighting caused me to justify my actions. They spent more time fighting with each other than they did paying attention to me.
- I went through puberty about the same time that I started looking at pornography online and found that pornography and masturbation felt really good.
- By age sixteen I found that I was intimidated by girls and each time I would try to talk with them I would do something stupid. That led me to pornography and masturbation because I figured at least I could fantasize about being accepted.

It is strange writing down these experiences. I am starting to see a lot of why I got so involved with pornography. It was very comforting to me, especially when I didn't have a close relationship with my parents. I also didn't have many close friends or at least I didn't think I did.

My first exposure to pornography was at age 12. I was over at Kendall Jones's house and his parents were gone. I remember the day very vividly. We were watching television and his older brother came into the room and asked if we were ready to be men. I didn't know what he was talking about. He put a video in the machine and the next thing I knew I was watching a pornographic video. I remember thinking I should not be watching this, but I was curious. In looking back I realize I was *so* curious. I could not pull my eyes off of it. I had been wondering about sex and now I was actually seeing it. I remember the excited feelings I had that day. I could not get my mind off of it the rest of that day. It is hard to describe the power of those feelings, but even today when I am looking at pornography I still feel those same intense feelings. You would think that I would get bored with it, but each time I see pornography I still get that feeling of excitement. Even now, just thinking about that experience, I get aroused. Perhaps these strong feelings come from the chemicals that are released into my system. I did not realize how powerful those chemicals were until we discussed them in counseling today. I know that I am addicted to that chemical high.

After my first exposure I didn't see pornography again until I was fourteen. I was home alone on our computer. I was looking up something for a science project and found some pornographic websites. That was the first time I saw pornography by myself. After that experience I found that it was easy to look at pornography. Over the next few months I found myself looking at pornography nearly every day. During that time I barely missed a day. Some days I would look at pornography in the morning before school and again after school. It became such a part of my life that I began thinking about it while at school. I would literally run home from school some days so that I would get more time viewing pornography before my mom came home from work. By age 16 I knew I had a problem. I couldn't stop looking for more than one week at a time. I didn't dare tell anyone because they wouldn't understand. I was embarrassed to talk about it.

At that time I didn't realize how much it was impacting me. I didn't hang out with other kids as much as I had in junior high school. I didn't feel comfortable talking with girls because I thought they were better than me. My guy friends talked about girls and sports and all I could think about was the pornography. It was my little secret. I tried to be social but I knew I was living a lie. I knew I was different than the other guys because they couldn't have a problem like I had. Little did I realize how many of them were actually looking at pornography too. Have I told you how much I hate pornography? Have I told you how much I hate myself because I have let it control my life for so many years?

Key points of what I learned today:

I guess I had never thought how much my childhood contributed to the development of my addiction. I am still afraid of getting close to others. I fear being rejected by others, so I often do not even try to get close to people. I need to discuss this with my therapist. I need to learn how to trust others and let others get close to me. I have had plenty of people try to get close to me but out of fear I push them away.

I need to learn how to turn to behaviors other than pornography when I am feeling alone or isolated. I have never had someone comfort me when I have felt sad or down. My parents were so involved in their own issues and they did not know how to reach out and help me. How can I learn to find comfort in things other than pornography when I am in emotional pain?

Things I am going to work on:

I need to learn how to develop healthy relationships with the people around me. I have relationships but they are mostly just surface relationships. I will talk with my therapist about ideas on how to do this.

I have reviewed my past two journal entries and feel like I have done well at reducing the fantasy and sexual thoughts that enter into my mind. However, I am starting to feel that gnawing feeling I feel when I have relapsed in the past. I think this is the beginning part of my relapse cycle. I don't know how to stop it. It scares me a little.

Therapist's comments:

Nice journal entry. Notice how your awareness about your own needs has increased. In this entry you realized that your experience in your family has limited your ability to connect with others in relationships. You have thwarted relationship opportunities because of your fears. Good awareness.

You also identified the need to find comfort in other things besides pornography. I would suggest that you make a list of things you can do that bring comfort to you. Then, when you are feeling emotionally down or frustrated, turn to that list of ideas.

The most important part of this journal entry may be your last awareness that you are starting to feel that gnawing feeling. That is a great awareness. However, now you need to come up with a plan to make it through these feelings. I would suggest you talk about it with a friend, family member, religious leader, or you can email or call me. Remember, your success will be winning this battle.

JOURNAL ENTRY: MAY 25, 2005
Dear Journal,

I am so frustrated. I relapsed last night and have been beating myself up over it. I did everything I had planned on doing. I realized I was experiencing the strong desire to view pornography and I even pulled out my game plan and reviewed it, but it didn't help. I justified getting on the computer because I needed to check my email. Once I got online in that state of mind, relapse was inevitable. I had been "Jonesing" for the past couple of days. I thought to myself, "I might as well get it over with." That seems to be a common thought I have when the strong cravings won't go away.

Now what do I do? I had been feeling so good about myself. I cannot deal with the feeling of failure. I have told myself over and over that I am done. It feels so helpless.

JOURNAL ENTRY: MAY 31, 2005
This last week has been bad. I didn't even finish my last journal entry because I didn't really care. I ended up relapsing three out of six days last week. I did as I usually do during this relapse: I binged for a few days and am now ready to try again. It is so frustrating. I want to stop, but this is hard.

I finally met with my therapist today. I learned some new things that I wish I had been aware of before my relapse. Perhaps the most important is that relapse is common. The therapist taught me some new stuff. It got a little complicated, but I think I understand it now, at least the basics. He told me about the precontemplation, contemplation, preparation, taking-action, and maintenance stages. He explained that I am in the preparation stage and that learning how to implement the skills is going to take time. I realize what he is saying is right. It is going to take time. He explained that alcoholics and drug addicts have 30, 60, and 90 day pins or awards because those are good goals to reach for. He also helped me realize that a good goal is focusing on things a day at a time rather than just thinking about never viewing pornography again.

He asked me to identify why I relapsed. Here's the story. I knew the internal pressure was building up and I even mentioned it in my journal entry from May 23. However, I didn't really care. I am so used to those feelings preceding relapse that I have quit trying to stop them. I have a belief that relapse is going to happen, so why fight it. I told my therapist this in our session and he asked me what I will do the next time that belief comes into my mind. At the time I didn't know, but I think I now know what I will do. The next time I am going to tell myself that I have to go through the withdrawal. I am going to recognize the feeling and tell myself that I had better be ready for the battle. I will also call up my friend John. He understands what I am going through and will be able to talk me through the tough time. I now understand that I relapsed because I didn't take this whole process serious.

The therapist asked me today how willing I am to give up pornography. He explained that giving up pornography is a lifestyle change. He asked me how much I am willing to sacrifice to overcome my pornography addiction. I hadn't thought about that before. It is a sacrifice. This has been such a big part of my life. But I'm not a quitter. I'm not going to let this beat me! I am going to stick with what I am learning in therapy. My therapist pointed out that most people who succeed in overcoming pornography addiction learn from their relapses.

Here's what I learned from this last series of relapses. First, I learned that I relapsed because I hadn't developed a good support system. When I was craving pornography I didn't have anyone to call so I just gave in. I read my game plan but I didn't follow it. I ignored all of the signs associated with my reaction sequence. These are the reasons why I didn't succeed.

The therapist also asked me what I was looking for when I relapsed. Was it to get a chemical high? Or was it to numb out stress or frustration? I think it was a little of both. I was under pressure at work and I felt like I deserved a break. However, I think more than anything I was just looking for a chemical high.

Now I need to keep up my awareness. I have learned a lot about myself over the past few weeks. I am going to succeed.

Key points of what I learned today:

I think I made big progress today. I understand much more about relapse. I realize it requires work to win this battle. I know that overcoming pornography isn't easy, but I thought I would go to a therapist and the solution would be easy. He helped me realize that I have to do a lot of the work. I understand that I need to have more awareness of what to do when the cravings are so strong. I also have to learn from a relapse rather than let myself get so caught up in my mistakes.

My therapist also taught me to have a backup mentality to abstinence—in other words, what happens if I slip up? He pointed out that slipping up can either be a learning experience or an excuse to binge. I am committed to *not* binging. He also quoted this statement from Dr. Stanton Peele, "If there is a relapse, getting down on yourself further exacerbates the problem. Self-loathing and despair lead to relapse. Remember that whenever you feel yourself sliding out of control that you have a choice."[1] I like that quote and have decided that I will write it down and keep it in my wallet.

Initially I was really down after my relapse, but now I am starting to understand that this is a process. I just need to keep learning. I really feel more optimistic.

Things I am going to work on:

I am going to break through the two-week pattern I have been succumbing to. I want to make it at least thirty days.

I want to learn more about the strong emotions I feel right before I relapse. The next time I am feeling those strong feelings I am going to write in my journal. I want to see if that will help me.

JOURNAL ENTRY: JUNE 2, 2005

I am making some progress. I feel more emotionally stable and calm. This is different than what I am used to after a relapse. I am really focusing on my emotions and understanding what I am feeling inside. It is amazing to me how much I was thinking about pornography. Now instead of dwelling on the thoughts that come into my mind, I am quickly changing my thoughts to things I have pre-planned. This is working well. For example, when a thought comes into my mind to view pornography I choose to think about the little child that I will have someday. I can see his brown eyes and brown hair. As I think about this experience, the strong feeling leaves. I am coming to realize that I can choose what I think about. That is a freeing thought.

During our last session my therapist taught me about identifying my emotions. I have been spending a lot of time evaluating my emotional ups and downs. I didn't realize how often I get sad or down. I also find that I have been bored a lot. When I think about it there isn't much of a reason for me to stay that way. There are so many exciting things I can think about and do. Staying away from pornography is one of them. I am excited about the idea of learning about my emotions and dealing with them in the moment rather than letting them get the best of me.

I have decided to create some guidelines and rules that I believe will lead to my success. Here are my rules:

1. Do not get online when you are feeling weak. If I feel a strong desire to view pornography I am going to read my book.
2. When I am alone I will not get on the computer. This rule has to stay in place until I am more confident. Why play with

fire? Eventually I may change this rule but not until I am more confident in my ability to succeed.

3. I will avoid watching television by myself after 11:00 P.M.

4. I am going to spend more time being social and interacting with family and friends.

Key points of what I learned today:

I need to stay focused on evaluating and understanding my emotions. I am excited by how aware I have become of my emotions lately. When I feel lonely I am realizing that I can turn to friends for help. Never before have I realized that my friends really do support me.

I also want to keep the rules and boundaries I have established. I will need to remind myself of them regularly.

Things I am going to work on:

As I review the things I have been working on I am going to keep the goal of writing down my emotions when I find myself struggling with the desire to relapse.

May 28 was the last day I relapsed. I know I haven't gone that long without it, but I feel more optimistic this time. I have the goal of breaking the two-week cycle I have been caught in.

JOURNAL ENTRY: JUNE 9, 2005

I am still doing well. This past week has been very busy at work. I am realizing that keeping busy has really helped with the battle. I am spending a lot less time in isolation. After work I come home and get involved in social activities or I invite some friends to go and do stuff. I didn't realize how much fun I was missing out on. In conjunction with keeping busy my therapist made a good point today. He taught me about the "productivity principle." He said that when people are being productive they are much less likely to relapse. He said that when people are engaged in positive and uplifting events and activities they have more focus and less cravings. This really fits with what I am doing right now in my life.

Normally this is the time when I start feeling a stronger build up, but I haven't felt it at all. This is encouraging. My therapist asked me why. I told him I think it is because I am really focusing on my emotions. If I feel down or frustrated I am trying to solve the problem rather than stay focused on the negative feelings. The solutions are really pretty easy if I just think about them. For example, my mom called today and was giving me a hard time about not visiting in a while. She also complained about my brother and sisters. She seems to always be so negative. The way she talks about my dad, I cannot believe that they were ever married. Now that they are divorced, I feel caught between the two of them. I cannot let myself focus on their problems. I cannot solve them. I used to use today's experience as an excuse to look at pornography. I would feel so frustrated by the conversation that I had with Mom that I would turn to pornography for comfort. Today I was frustrated, but I quickly thought to myself that my mom probably isn't going to change so I had better learn to cope with her behavior in a positive way. I actually did something positive on the phone with her. I said, "Mom, I want you to know that I know how hard it has been on you since you and Dad divorced." I didn't say anything else, I just listened. She didn't know what to say other than, "Thanks!"

I am feeling more upbeat than I have felt in a while. My therapist encouraged me to start making some short, medium, and long-range goals. I will need to think about what I would like for goals. I have never been much of a goal-oriented person, but I am going to try. I really want to kick this addiction. You know, the strangest thing is happening inside of me. I am really starting to feel hope. I hope I am not getting too cocky, but I really am excited about the things I am learning about myself.

Key points of what I learned today:

More than anything I am more optimistic than I have been for a long time. This is the time when I have to be careful so I am taking extra precautions. I am keeping busy and maintaining good social relationships. For the first time in my life, I feel like I have friends. My therapist invited me to talk with John about being an accountability partner. He wants me to start reporting my goals and personal expectations with him. I can talk to him when I am having a hard time. I will report to John at least once a month. At first I thought, no way! It would be too embarrassing, which is why I have kept this a secret most of my life. But the goal is worth it, and I will make myself vulnerable to succeed. My therapist encouraged me to talk with John for at least one year about my goals and progress. He indicated that a good accountability partner can help during the six month to one year period of time. He read to me from Dr. Carnes's book about relapse being more common for sex addicts between the six-month and one-year mark. I think long-term accountability is a good idea.

Things I am going to work on:

My goal is to talk with John about being an accountability partner. I will tell him I would like to talk with him at least once a month for a year about my goals and challenges related to pornography.

JOURNAL ENTRY: JUNE 30, 2005

It has been a while since I last wrote in my journal. Things have been going extremely well. I am confident in my awareness and ability to fight this battle with pornography. It has been one month and two days since I last viewed pornography. This is the longest I have gone in over a year without viewing pornography.

I have learned that when I am busy I have little to no problem with the cravings. I am most vulnerable when I have free time with nothing planned. As a result I have started to plan my days in advance to make sure I keep busy and engaged in positive activities. I have decided to volunteer at a local homeless shelter on Wednesday afternoons. This has been a great experience and it makes me feel good about myself.

After talking with my therapist I have come to realize that I am missing something major in my life. I am missing a female companion. I have had a hard time admitting that, but if I look deep inside of myself, I realize I am very lonely. I think that is what led to many of my relapses in the past. With this awareness I am working to develop better relationships with the women around me. I know that if I am going to succeed I have to feel more comfortable about myself. My therapist asked me to identify the beliefs I have developed about dating and relationships. Here's my list:

- No girl would want me because of my involvement with pornography.
- I am not good enough for the type of girl that I would like to be with.
- I have seen women as objects in the past and I am concerned that I will treat women as objects.

After writing these beliefs down, it hit me: I don't believe them anymore. I used to really believe those things and I've had a bunch of bad relationships as a result. My therapist encouraged me to start thinking about what a healthy relationship would be like between a man and woman. How would they treat each other? What would they not do in their relationship? It is interesting to note that I am starting to see how my therapist has me thinking about the things I have always wanted in my life, but have never thought I would achieve.

Finally, today I want to put my goals down.

Short-term goals:

- I will remain sober and make it to 90 days. I am over 30 days now and I am feeling good.
- I will start meeting new women with whom I can develop friendships.
- I am going to start exercising three days a week by lifting weights or jogging.

Mid-range goals:

- I will stay away from pornography for 180 days.

- I will ask three different girls out on a date. On those dates I am going to work on getting to know more about them and the things they like and do not like. I will not discuss sexual things or make sexual jokes.
- I am going to run in a 5K race.

Long-term goals:

- I will avoid pornography for one full year.
- I will continue developing dating relationships with the hope of getting serious. I know that I cannot make a goal to be serious with anyone, but I am going to continue to develop my relationship skills. I will read at least three books to develop this skill.
- I am going to build up my endurance so that I can run a marathon.

Key points of what I learned today:

I am starting to see my progress and my future. When I was heavily involved in pornography I could hardly think about anything but pornography. Now I am focusing on things I want to do in the future. It is nice to write down my goals. I may add upon them as time goes by, but for now they will be my focus.

Things I am going to work on:

After reviewing the things I was going to work on from my last entry I realized that I didn't report that John has agreed to be my accountability partner. We will be talking this next week. I will share my goals with him.

I want to start reading a book on developing good dating and relationship skills.

JOURNAL ENTRY: JULY 14, 2005

I think I need to journal today. I am going through some withdrawal symptoms. I am edgy and irritable. I have been feeling more moody than

I have been in a while. I am really having a strong craving this evening. I am alone with the day off from work tomorrow. As soon as I recognized these feelings inside, I decided to write in my journal. I am really craving pornography. I haven't felt this way for about six weeks. I recently learned to go through an internal game plan that I developed with my therapist. First, I have done well with recognizing the craving. Now I need to identify the source. The source is being alone with nothing to do. What is the outcome if I don't change my circumstances? I will give in. What would happen if I choose to give in? I will feel bad, as usual. I will get the temporary high but I don't want to do that. If I don't give in what will happen? I will be better off. I can do this. I don't have to look at pornography. Who can I call? John is gone. I should have had a back up plan tonight. Okay, what is my game plan? I am going to go jogging and then go and get some ice cream. If the cravings have not subsided, I will go and visit my friend Alison.

JOURNAL ENTRY: JULY 28, 2005

It has now been two months since I last viewed pornography. I am feeling good. I just reviewed my first entry and it was cool to see how much progress I have made in the last two months. I know that I am not out of the woods, my experience two weeks ago taught that, but I am succeeding. The challenges haven't been too bad the past couple of weeks. I continue to identify my emotions and cravings before they build up. I am also keeping close with John when things get rough. I have developed a rule that if my cravings are really strong, I call him up and tell him. He talks me through them.

JOURNAL ENTRY: AUGUST 4, 2005

One thing I haven't mentioned a lot in this process is the spiritual help that I have received lately. I have been focusing more on spiritual things like reading and praying, and this has given me great strength. A few weeks ago my therapist taught me about three levels of awareness. The first level is where I was when I first started therapy. I never thought about why I did what I did. It was what he called safety. Then over time I have learned to ask myself more questions. I have started to think about why I do what I do. When I feel frustrated or down I have started really thinking about the reasons why. This level of awareness has really helped me fight this battle with pornography. My therapist calls this type of awareness level-two awareness. He also taught me about a third level. This is a mindset in which you can receive feedback from a higher source (God). He explained that when I am in a mindset where I am pondering and thinking about how to solve my problems I am more likely to receive thoughts and feelings from a higher source, especially if I will listen and write down the thoughts that come to my mind. He indicated that when we are at level-two awareness if we are willing to let our minds and hearts think about solutions, they will come. This is a concept that makes sense to me. He said that most people live at level one. They just live their lives without ever really thinking about why they are living life the way they are.

I must admit that I feel much more spiritual now than I did two months ago. I feel like my progress is accepted by God and He has really supported me through these past couple of months. While talking about my spirituality with my therapist he gave me the following quotes: "Real life is response to the best within us. To be alive only to appetite, pleasure, pride, money-making, and not to goodness and kindness, purity and love, poetry, music, flowers, stars, God and eternal hopes, is to deprive oneself of the real joy of living,"[2] and "Character is built into the spiritual fabric of personality hour by hour, day by day, year by year in much the same deliberate way that physical health is built into the body."[3]

I should mention that I have run in a couple of 5K runs and am doing well in them. I enjoy the runs and I am finding that I feel good about myself when I compete and do well. This is something that I didn't know about myself.

JOURNAL ENTRY: AUGUST 28, 2005

I decided that I needed to write today. It has officially been three months (90 days) since my last relapse. I must admit that it hasn't been easy.

I have had many days that I simply wanted to give in but something inside of me said "no more." I have continued talking with John and my therapist. I talk with John at least once a week. I am only seeing my therapist once a month.

Something exciting has happened to me, I have met a woman (Julie) who I am very interested in getting to know. We have been spending a lot of time together lately and this has really helped me fight off the temptations. In fact, I haven't felt this good in a long time. In my free time I think about Julie. I guess I will talk with my therapist about her during our next session on September 15. I wonder how to deal with her and my past involvement with pornography.

I am surprised at how easy it has been lately. I haven't had any desire to view pornography. I have been so excited about this relationship that I haven't been able to think about anything else. I am a little surprised at how easy this seems. I guess I feel more confident in myself since I haven't seen pornography in three months.

I just reviewed some of my goals and have decided that I am doing well on most of them. Here's a list of things that I would still like to work on.
Things I am going to work on:

I read two books on dating and relationships. I first read Dr. Neil Clark Warren's book, *Date or Soul Mate?*[4] Next I took Dr. Skinner's online relationship test for singles.[5] These helped me identify specific things I need to work on in relationships. I also made a list of things that I wanted in a relationship with a woman. I realized that I need to work on better communicating my emotions with the people I date. I often feel emotions but keep them bottled up inside. Next, I need to listen and ask more questions. These are two areas that I am working on in my relationship with Julie.

I have realized that I probably need to talk with Julie about my involvement with pornography. The other day we were watching TV and a news channel discussed children and teenagers being involved in pornography. She expressed clear frustration with the pornography industry and those who promote it. I am a little scared to talk with her about this. However, I know I need to talk with her. I am afraid that she will end our relationship. I guess I will wait and talk with my therapist about this before I talk with her.

JOURNAL ENTRY: SEPTEMBER 15, 2005

Things with Julie are still going really well. We have been spending every free moment we have together. I must admit that my feelings for Julie have stirred up strong sexual feelings inside of me. I haven't viewed pornography, but it hasn't been easy because of how close we are getting. The more intimately we kiss the more difficult it is for me to turn off those feelings, especially when I am by myself. However, I haven't given in because of how much I respect and want to be with her. She is the best woman I have ever dated.

I talked with my therapist today. We discussed how I could talk with Julie about my experience. I was reluctant, but my therapist discussed the importance of having her on my team. He helped me realize that this battle will be ongoing and if I have accountability with her I will be much less likely to relapse. His "no more secrets" policy makes sense. We role played what I could say and how she might respond. He pointed out that her response would teach me a lot about our relationship. He helped me see that she would be hurt, but he also showed me how honesty could strengthen our relationship. Here are some of the key points he brought up.

1. Honesty will help her trust me in the long run. I haven't viewed any pornography in over three months and I have been going to counseling. This may help her trust me.
2. Julie will likely be hurt and I need to understand this and not be critical or judgmental of her response. She may need time to decide if she wants to pursue this relationship with me. My therapist pointed out that many women don't end the relationship but they want openness and honesty. They want to talk

about it. If Julie is willing to talk I will need to be ready to communicate with her.

3. If Julie is willing she can be one of my accountability partners. I don't know how she will respond to this, but I like this idea. She and I can talk about anything, except for this. If I can talk with her about my struggles with pornography, I think we will be able to talk about and resolve issues we encounter in the future.

4. I also need to be prepared if Julie chooses to not continue this relationship. If she needs time I need to give it to her. If she wants to end it completely, I will need to increase my communication with John and my therapist. I hope this doesn't happen, but I cannot control her response. I need to remember that I have been making progress and so there is nothing more I can do.

JOURNAL ENTRY: SEPTEMBER 18, 2005

I talked with Julie tonight. I didn't have any idea of how she would respond. I was scared to death. She expressed a lot of hurt and disappointment. However, she did appreciate that I told her. I explained to her all of the things I have been doing to overcome this addiction. She seemed pleased by my efforts, but told me she needed some time to work through her own feelings. I don't know what to expect from her at this point. She told me she wanted a day or two to think about things and then we would talk. Although we ended on a good note, she was not as affectionate as she has been. I tried to listen and understand as my counselor discussed. I think I did well in explaining myself, but I am very nervous. What if she decides that she doesn't want a relationship with me? I honestly don't know how I will respond. I cannot blame her if she doesn't want to pursue a relationship, as she has such strong feelings about pornography.

Tonight she told me that one of her sisters married a man who was struggling with pornography addiction. This is the first time that she opened up with me about this issue. This may be her biggest worry. Her sister's husband has been involved for years but has been doing it behind his wife's back. She found out six months ago and has been devastated. I don't know how this will impact Julie's decision but it does concern me.

I am sick inside. My insides are turning and I feel upset. I don't think I will be able to sleep much tonight. Julie told me that she would call me. I think she will need some time working through her emotions.

I just called John to discuss my experience. He was supportive. He sure has been a good friend. Now it is a waiting game. The interesting thing right now is that I have *no* desire to view pornography. In fact, I am beginning to feel a very strong dislike for it. The therapist told me this might happen. I look at my former self and realize that I was caught in a nasty web. I am starting to make it out, but have to remind myself that this is an ongoing battle.

Now it is a waiting game. I just hope and pray that Julie will give me a chance. My therapist told me that if she is interested in working on the relationship that I should bring her to our next session.

JOURNAL ENTRY: SEPTEMBER 21, 2005

I just completed the longest three days of my life. I didn't hear back from Julie until this evening. I was very anxious. She told me that she had given this serious consideration and that she was still interested in pursuing a relationship. She explained her initial feelings of hurt, distrust, and questioning whether she really knew me at all. Then after experiencing those feelings she told me how much she appreciated my openness and willingness to talk with her. This is what saved our relationship. She told me that had she found out some other way she would have ended the relationship because she promised herself that she would only be with someone who was honest with her.

What a relief. She was more affectionate tonight than on Sunday night, but she still isn't completely comfortable. My therapist warned me that this would take time. Julie asked me about my therapy and I explained to her some of the things that the therapist has taught me. She seemed interested so I invited her to come with me. She was pleased with that so we will attend the next session together.

JOURNAL ENTRY: SEPTEMBER 23, 2005

I didn't realize how hard this would be on Julie. She seemed so strong on Wednesday when we discussed her decision, but she is still extremely hurt. Tonight she told me that she spends a lot of time worrying if I am going to relapse. I didn't know how to respond other than tell her that I have been doing my best. I really didn't know how to comfort her. She wants to trust me, but is afraid of getting hurt. I found myself getting defensive tonight. I wanted to tell her to trust me. I wanted this whole thing to be over so we could move on. These are things I obviously wasn't thinking about when I was so involved in pornography. I never considered how actions of months ago would impact someone who I wanted to be close to.

I realize now that this is going to be harder than I thought. It is going to take more work and energy. I am going to need to be patient with Julie. It is on nights like tonight that I find myself thinking of how easy it would be to just turn away from this relationship, but that is running from the problem. As difficult as tonight was in dealing with Julie's anger and frustration, I realize I need to learn how to help her. I felt so helpless. I hate creating pain for others.

I suppose in the past I would have taken an experience like tonight and said forget the whole thing and turned to pornography. That thought did come to my mind tonight but I was able to recognize it quickly and tell myself that would put an end to my relationship with Julie and I am not willing to compromise what I want with her. I realize how much I like spending time with her. Thank goodness we get to talk with my therapist on Monday.

JOURNAL ENTRY: SEPTEMBER 26, 2005

We met with my therapist today. He helped Julie understand more about pornography addiction. He explained to her the challenges ahead. Here's the list he gave us:

Things to watch for:

- Secrets—watch for things that do not make sense.

- Observe emotions—pay close attention to the emotions of the addict. If he is more grumpy, irritable, or overly frustrated for no apparent reason, talk about it.
- Late nights and unexplained absences.
- Lack of closeness or connection in the relationship.
- Being overly aggressive or physical in the sexual aspect of the relationship.
- Change in attitude and openness in discussing pornography related issues.
- Downplaying the importance of getting help.

He also discussed things we could do to increase our communication about pornography. He talked about the importance of discussing my goals and the rules and guidelines I have established with Julie. She was interested in talking with me about them. I am hopeful that we will be able to discuss these together. It may be a little difficult at first, but it may help us regain some of the trust Julie lost.

Julie told my counselor about her fear of relapse. He made an interesting point when he said that most people hurt their marriages when they maintain and keep secrets. He indicated that many of the couples who end up divorced are the ones who are unwilling to discuss their issues with each other. I feel safe with Julie. She hasn't been judgmental, which has helped me open up to her. We discussed the importance of me being open with her if I am feeling the craving to view pornography. She told me that she wanted to be a support for me at those times. I am going to try this with her instead of John the next time I am struggling with the cravings.

I am still tempted periodically, but not nearly as much as I was in the past. My therapist explained that one way to observe how much pornography is impacting you is by how much time you spend thinking about it. He asked me what percentage of the time I used to spend thinking about pornography. I told him at the worst probably 50 percent of my free time was spent thinking about or viewing pornography. Then he asked me how much

I think about it now. My answer was maybe three to five percent. I really don't think about it that much anymore. This really helped me see the progress that I have made. I think it helped Julie understand as well. She asked if she could ask me how much I have been thinking about pornography. I said that would be fine.

JOURNAL ENTRY: DECEMBER 30, 2005

The year is almost over and I have continued to do well. Things with Julie are going really well. I just wanted to report that I am doing well. I have reviewed my goals and have realized that I have met most of them. I am now setting goals for staying away from pornography for one year. I continue to have times that I feel the craving to give in, but I am quick to get away from the computer or TV when this occurs. My New Year's goals are listed below.

- Keep focused on my work. I have really been doing well at work. I didn't realize how much pornography was taking me away from being effective until I stepped back and looked at what I was doing. I am making good progress and expect I may get a promotion this upcoming year.
- I want to stay honest with Julie in all things. She is regaining her trust in me and I want to keep it that way. We have had some struggles with communication and I have held back from being totally honest with her at times because I was afraid she would be overly critical. However, we have talked about her need for openness and my need for her to tell me when she is struggling with being overly critical.
- I am going to continue to avoid late night TV and Internet usage. I have installed an Internet filter on my computer and it reports to Julie all of my Internet activity. This has really helped her relax since she knows what sites I am visiting online.
- I will keep exercising. I had a good year of exercise and I think this really helped me stay focused on reaching my goals. I ran

a marathon the first week in October. That was a great experience. I have learned that goals have really helped me stay focused.

Well, it has now been seven months since I last viewed pornography. It hasn't been easy, but I have been succeeding. I like how I feel about myself. Eight months ago I wouldn't have thought I could feel this way. Now I just want to keep this up. I am excited for the future since I know I can succeed.

Chapter 10:
Living the Lifestyle that Leads to Recovery

It is exciting to watch the developing lifestyle of individuals who are in recovery. Hope, fun, energy, and the pursuit of dreams become a part of everyday life. This vitality and return of hope for life is difficult to explain to the person who is just starting down the path to recovery. When I tell clients that they are going to have to develop a new lifestyle in order to create a lasting change, many wonder what I mean.

Stuart's story is a perfect example of developing a new lifestyle. When he was most heavily involved in pornography he was grumpy and moody. He didn't like being at his job, he stayed up into the early morning, and he would consequently be late for work. His employers would pass him over for promotions because he was apathetic toward his responsibilities. If his employers could have found reason to fire him, they would have. His wife was also frustrated with him. She had started threatening that if he didn't start dealing with his problems she would leave him—and he realized that someday she might. He knew he needed to change if he was going to have the life he had always wanted.

Pornography had taken over his life. When we met he didn't hide anything. He was very contrite. He wanted help, but didn't know where to start. Over the next few months he made tremendous progress. Eventually he took a new job with more opportunities. His relationship with his wife began to improve. He started talking about his goals and dreams. As I reviewed his progress, I realized that this book needed one more chapter. This chapter outlines the principles that guided his recovery, and others like him, who are also successfully beating this addiction. These principles will be highlighted as follows.

COMMITMENT TO INTEGRITY

At the crux of every recovering addict's story is a deep commitment to integrity. By definition, integrity means being complete or whole. It also encompasses being honest, loyal, and committed. In the early stages of change a majority of the people with whom I have worked have told me that they struggle with honesty or being committed. They are basically honest people but this one area plagues them. It is very hard for them to openly admit their level of involvement in pornography. Many minimize their exposure and consequently are not honest with themselves and others. They have a hard time telling their true story.

On the other hand, those in recovery have learned that telling their story, without minimizing or holding anything back, actually helps set them free. They learn to be comfortable sharing their long-held secret with others. They realize that if they are going to heal they need to be completely honest with themselves and others. One way to identify those who are recovering is to observe their level of openness and honesty. One who is well down the path towards recovery has come to be at ease telling his story.

For many years, deception, hiding, lying, late nights, and excuses filled their lives. Now, while in recovery, they tell their story. They talk of years of making up lies and excuses so they could stay home and view pornography. They tell of late nights at the office solely for the purpose of viewing pornography. They explain that their post office box was for the purpose of receiving pornographic videos. In anguish they explain how they have spent thousands of dollars on pornography.

One of the prerequisites for sharing a story is finding someone who understands and is not judgmental. Those who have a safe environment to talk find that others understand that pornography is an addiction and are not as critical of their behavior. They find the needed support and care on which they need to rely. In many instances this is a caring spouse, friend, or religious leader. With a positive environment around them they begin the process of recovery. In telling their stories they have no more secrets.

With these secrets out they begin to feel good about themselves. They have learned that honesty and telling the truth actually sets them free.

As part of their healing they have learned to be emotionally honest with themselves. They learn to recognize their own emotional state (e.g., upset, tired, bored, irritated, angry, etc.) and deal with it rather than turn to misbehavior such as pornography. They have learned to identify the cravings to view pornography and admit this to themselves. They have learned with pinpoint accuracy when they are more vulnerable to relapse because they can openly acknowledge when they are weak. This type of honesty is what I call emotional integrity or being honest with one's own emotions. Those who have learned to have this type of integrity have developed a skill that leads to success.

There are many ways they have learned to be honest. They can talk with others or write in a journal. They can process (meaning think through) their emotions (good and bad) in their own minds. The lifestyle of the successful is one of complete honesty. They are emotionally honest with themselves and others. Their honesty translates into other areas of their life. They become more reliable and dependable in what they do and say. Others begin to trust them. As a result they become more confident. Dr. David Viscott described the outcome of integrity when he said, "If you lived honestly, your life would heal itself." [1]

Some of the attitudes that accompany the principle of integrity include:

- No more secrets.
- Being emotionally honest and truthful in all dealings.
- Recognition that a lie is any communication given with the intent to deceive.
- Being the same in public as you are in private.
- Taking responsibility for any problems created and, to the extent possible, trying to make them right.
- Keeping commitments unless released from them.

Those who have learned to be honest with themselves and others are good candidates for long lasting change and healing. They begin to have more meaningful relationships. Once they embrace this lifestyle, going back to pornography becomes scary and abhorrent to them.

VALUING SELF AND SHOWING GENUINE COMPASSION FOR OTHERS

One of the fundamental elements behind true recovery is believing in self. When pornography and other addictive behaviors overtake a person's life, negative beliefs are often formed about self-worth and value. Individuals who have been caught in the trap of pornography often feel out of control and consequently struggle with feelings of low self-worth. However, as healing begins and recovery begins to take place, beliefs about self and others begin to change. Susan L. Taylor, in her book *Lessons in Living,* wrote, "When we become expert at loving and caring for ourselves, we feel healthy, centered, and strong. We don't need escape from our reality through shopping, eating, drinking, drugging, or losing ourselves in abusive relationships. We feel warm and safe within ourselves."[2]

Individuals who learn the importance of valuing self realize that their addiction has prevented them from finding joy and happiness in life. They often become so critical of self that they lose sight of their own goodness and worth. Feeling caught in their addictive behaviors they often loathe self and feel like others are too critical of them or don't understand them. They are more prone to become frustrated with anything that requires their focus and attention. As they begin the recovery process they go through a painful awareness of how their actions have hurt themselves and others.

As time progresses and additional healing occurs, these individuals begin to genuinely find true value for self. This is an exciting process to watch in those who are recovering. They begin to talk with more hope and excitement. Their actions demonstrate that they are valuing themselves because they are engaging in positive and productive activities. They often become more social and engage in activities that make them feel good about themselves.

There is also a stark difference in the attitudes about others in those who are recovering and those still caught in pornography. Those who are moving toward long-term recovery demonstrate more compassion for people. They make people feel comfortable around them. They are not pushy. They make you feel better about yourself when you are with them. They don't judge you, but they encourage you to be better by what they do, not what they say. They are positive. People love being around those who are good at sending value and affirming the worth of others.

Below are a few of the beliefs of those who affirm their own worth and send value to others.

- All persons, including self, are of infinite worth.
- Behavior, for the most part, is learned.
- Misbehavior is almost always a symptom of some other problem (e.g., pornography is an escape from emotional frustration or loneliness).
- Behavior is almost invariably belief linked.

Those who genuinely believe these statements often find themselves wanting to understand others rather than be critical or judgmental. Remember the power that beliefs play in a person's mind. If we believe we or others are bad we will act accordingly. If we don't feel valued by others and society we will be more likely to engage in addictive behaviors.

It is also important to keep in mind that most people develop addictions and other problems for reasons that most of us do not understand. Only when we try to understand others and how they feel and think do we really see them for who they are. Understanding how others got to where they are in life can often help us resist the desire to be overly critical of ourselves and to misjudge others. Those who learn to value self and others genuinely believe in the goodness of people, including themselves.

Those who are in recovery value self by learning to avoid their addictive behavior. As they develop inner confidence they are more prone to reach out and help others and they appreciate all of those who helped them along the way. Dr. Carnes shares a great story about a recovered sex addict who held a ten-year celebration party for his friends who helped him remain clean and sober. During the party, two thoughts came to mind. First, how the people around him had helped him from the beginning and, second, of his own progress that he could call a party in his own honor without feeling shame or guilt.[3]

Those who are in recovery feel more in charge of their lives. They are less likely to hold back or shy away from challenges. This gives them more of a feeling that they can control their lives. One reason, I believe, that addicts don't like themselves is because their feelings are out of control. When they regain control of their lives they feel an increase in their own worth and subsequently are more likely to engage in life and relationships with more confidence. Thus, the power of valuing self and others is key in those who are in recovery.

COMMITMENT TO GROWTH

Either we grow or we regress. It is hard to stay stagnant for extended periods of time. Those who do are genuinely frustrated with their lives. A clear sign of those in recovery is the development of new skills and an increase in positive relationships. Growth refers to development, creativity, and new opportunities. Josh described this feeling, saying, "My world is so different today. I have returned to things that I used to like to do and I have developed new hobbies. But most importantly, I am being a better dad and husband."

Growth brings a positive feeling and increases our energy. I learned this lesson one day when I was sitting in my office answering phone calls and avoiding the things I should have been doing. After an hour of wasting time I heard a colleague come into the office just as excited as could be. He had just finished his book and was very upbeat and energetic. At that time my initial reaction was jealousy. I thought about how much time I was wasting and about the things I was avoiding. That experience changed my life. I realized that there is a principle behind being productive. I call this the productivity principle. The principle is this: If we are engaged in positive activities that build us up and help us achieve goals we are more likely to feel good about ourselves. The result is that our inner energy increases and we are more likely to engage in uplifting activities.

The other end of the productivity principle is being idle or lazy. As I have explored this principle with my clients I have learned that many of them relapse when they are bored or are avoiding things they should be doing. Understanding this has helped me identify that I need to be engaged in positive activities. I have also learned that I can always find something productive to do. When I teach clients this principle, many have come back to me with fun examples of what they are doing to be productive. For example, one client decided to write music. A few days later he sent me a piece of music he had composed and played. Engaging in positive activities is a great way to avoid unhealthy behaviors.

Another element with growth is learning to be in an environment where one can grow. In some environments it is virtually impossible to grow. John's wife was constantly on his case about his work and how little he was helping around the house. He couldn't do anything right. He learned to escape by turning to pornography. After being yelled at he would always justify looking at pornography. As we began talking I realized that his environment was contributing to his addiction. I pointed this out with a clear emphasis on separating his addiction to pornography from his relationship with his wife. I told him that I do not believe it is right to blame an addiction on a spouse. Becoming addicted is a personal choice. However, his environment was so negative he didn't know where else to turn for respite from the constant attacks he was getting from his wife.

As we discussed his pattern of turning to pornography after an argument, we identified new behaviors in which he could engage to avoid turning to pornography. As he learned these new coping mechanisms, he realized his wife had a problem. Previously he couldn't see her anger problem because he felt so guilty because of his addiction. Soon he was able to discuss with her his need to be in a relationship where he wasn't constantly being put down or ridiculed.

The lesson from this experience taught me that it is critical that clients learn to identify their type of environment. When they learn this concept it is not uncommon for them to change that environment. Some change jobs. Others move their computer or TV out of their individual rooms. Still others begin focusing on developing relationships with people who do not tell sexual jokes or send them pornography over the Internet.

Watching how people grow during the recovery process is enjoyable. Growth is fundamental to long-term recovery. Some of the areas in which I have seen growth in clients are listed below:

- Job promotions
- Increased family interaction (e.g., spending more time with family and spouse)
- More involvement in social events and activities
- Participation in exercise (e.g., running, weights)
- Improved grades

One of my favorite sayings is "Life is too short not to enjoy it." Those who are in recovery develop a passion for growth because it brings them hope and more reasons to enjoy life. Are you growing or not?

COMMITMENT TO AGENCY

As humans we will do almost anything to be free. We insist on being able to choose and make choices without being controlled or manipulated. The ironic thing about addiction is that it actually limits our choices. When a grown man cries in my office as he describes his challenge of overcoming a pornography addiction, he clearly feels restricted because of his habit. Ask anyone who has suffered from an addiction about the power of his cravings and the internal drive he feels when thoughts of viewing pornography come into his mind—he will express strong feelings of hopelessness and helplessness. This is not freedom of choice.

On the other end of the addiction continuum is agency or feeling free to choose. As pornography addicts move toward freedom they realize how limited their life has become. They begin to see how they have isolated themselves from family and friends. They learn how their job has suffered. They also see how much of their life has been spent in a fantasy world. In regaining freedom they turn toward a lifestyle of choices. They begin to explore and see more options for their life.

Timothy described this by telling me his personal story. He explained how he used to think about ways he could find pornography on the Internet. He described spending hours a day fantasizing about pornography when he was doing other things. Then when he had the opportunity he would spend as much time as he could viewing websites and downloading video clips. As he began recovering he started spending more time planning for road trips and hikes he would take. This transitioned into spending more time finding good hiking trails. Soon he found many other things besides pornography that he could spend time thinking about. His mind was free for the first time in years to ponder and think about things that would lift him up rather than keep him trapped in an activity that ended up with feelings of remorse, guilt, and shame.

Agency, or the drive to be free, is inside all of us. However, many who are addicted to pornography do not feel free. In fact, it is common for men and women to explain to me that they want to change but they do not know how. This begs the question of how much agency someone really has if he does not know how to do something differently. The answer, I believe, is that most people who are addicted to pornography do not know how to be free from this addiction. Therefore, the solution is knowledge. This is why it is so critical to learn the right skills to overcome this addiction. We can only be free when we realize we have choices.

Once individuals learn they have choices the question then is: Which will give the more abundant life—pampering our physical nature or developing our spiritual selves?[4] Those who are in recovery learn to recognize that pornography is simply covering up emotional pain or it is fulfilling a need for excitement. With this knowledge many choose to be free from these natural responses. They identify new and healthy ways of dealing with emotional pain and they learn how to fill their need for excitement with activities that are not addictive. This is true freedom.

COMMITMENT TO TRUSTING YOUR INSTINCTS AND YOUR OWN INTUITIVE RESPONSES

We are spiritual beings who in times of need turn to a higher source for strength and support. That is why so many addiction groups use a twelve-step program, founded on spiritually based principles. Addicts use these twelve steps to heal from seemingly impossible to overcome addictions. For many, learning to turn to God is difficult because they feel like they are unworthy of God's love. Some feel they have no right to ask God for assistance in overcoming their addiction. However, those who are in recovery learn that turning to God can offer great assistance to them while in need.

David O. McKay once said, "Generally there is in man a divinity which strives to push him onward and upward. We believe that this power within him is the spirit that comes from God. . . . At sometime in his life, every man is conscious of a desire to come in touch with the Infinite. His spirit reaches out for God. This sense of feeling is universal, and all men ought to be, in deepest truth, engaged in the same great work—the search for and the development of spiritual peace and freedom." [5]

Engaging in the process of spiritual healing is an important journey for each of us. It requires that one learns to trust impressions and become more in touch with emotions. Getting in touch with these emotions and learning to trust in a higher being is invaluable in the healing process. Those who engage in efforts to become in touch with the Infinite learn to trust their instincts and God-sent intuitive responses almost automatically.

One client described it this way, "When I am willing to submit my inner drive for instant satisfaction to the pursuit of spiritual or higher feelings, I realize I can achieve a longer lasting high. So when I feel a powerful inner drive to view pornography, I can either get a quick fix or I can step back and think of my real goals in life." Describing the process of learning to control our instant impulses, David O. McKay also said, "Indulgence in appetites and desires of the physical man satisfy but for the moment and may lead to unhappiness, misery, and possible degradation; spiritual achievements give 'joy not to be repented of.'"[6]

Some of the most powerful spiritual highs come from battling with cravings that are so strong that the only option is to white-knuckle it through the challenging withdrawal symptoms. Those who endure such times often look back and realize that only God could have helped them through the fight.

EMOTIONS AND SPIRITUALITY

During the recovery process emotions are often close to the surface. Allowing oneself to feel emotion is a big step in the process of spiritual healing. When I first meet with clients they tell me that they feel numb and out of touch with their own emotions. Over time as they remove themselves from pornography they get back in touch with their emotions, which allows them to feel internal promptings and feelings.

Emotions are also helpful in that they are internal regulators that tell us when something is not quite right in our lives. For example, if a person is having a strong craving to view pornography, learning to identify this feeling as soon as it is felt is very important. While identifying such a powerful internal feeling many of my clients have learned to take this emotion and seek help from God to either remove the desire or to give them the strength to engage in a more positive and healthy behavior.

Here's how the process works: A person feels a desire to view pornography. This creates an emotion that the person in recovery has learned to deal with as soon as it comes into the mind. The second step is to ask for help from a higher source. The third step is to ask questions such as, "How can I get rid of this craving?" Seeking a solution is a valuable step when it comes to the inner workings of the human mind. If the mind can see a different solution it creates an alternative pathway rather than the worn out mental trail that has allowed it to view pornography so often in the past. I have seen many clients use this three-step approach. The key is identifying the emotion and then looking to God for help in coming up with a strategy to fight off the craving.

The three steps identified above involve learning to trust one's own internal instincts. The recognition and awareness of the emotion triggers the mind to take action and then look for a solution. This internal processing buys time for the mind to evaluate and decide on a response. While doing this repeatedly, solutions can come into the mind from a higher source who strengthens in times of need and provides peace during trials. Those who tap into this eternal source find hope that overcoming pornography addiction is indeed possible and real.

THE JOY OF LIVING A NEW LIFESTYLE

The bridge for overcoming pornography addiction has been created. Others have gone before you. The ideas and suggestions found in this book are tools that others have used to succeed. As you implement them, the joy of living a new lifestyle will be instilled in your heart and mind. You will find your life to be more complete and whole. Remember, this is a journey that takes time and effort. Mistakes may occur along the way, but as you begin to live the lifestyle that leads to recovery, you will find that life will have more meaning. You will find yourself and realize you are better than you think.

May God bless you in your journey.

Appendix A

Stimulus:_____

_____

_____

Thought:_____

_____

_____

Emotion:_____

_____

_____

Chemical Release:_____

_____

_____

Body Language:_____

_____

_____

Second Thought:_____

_____

_____

Belief:_____

_____

_____

Behavior:_____

_____

_____

Appendix B:
Assessing Pornography Addiction Test

The Assessing Pornography Addiction test was developed to help evaluate your level of involvement in pornography by exploring seven different areas associated with pornography use. Areas include:

Your history — The extent of your involvement with pornography (current and past)

Intensity — The amount your mind is preoccupied with thoughts, feelings, and emotions related to pornography. It also looks at how your involvement in pornography may have progressed over time. Finally, this section identified risks that you may be taking related to your involvement with pornography.

Impulse Control — Explores your ability to deal with cravings/temptations and the power that they have on you in difficult times.

Consequences — Identifies areas of your life that your involvement with pornography may have hurt or harmed in some way.

Coping Strategies — Evaluates the extent that you turn to pornography to cope with challenges you face.

Mental Health — Explores areas of your mental health (depression, loneliness, and guilt) related to viewing pornography.

Overall Well-Being — Explores your overall level of happiness and life satisfaction.

You'll be asked questions to identify the extent that pornography is influencing your life. Once you've completed your assessment, you'll be given a level of involvement and specific suggestions to help you.

Note: This assessment is intended for individuals who are actively viewing pornography. If you have reached a level of sobriety in your recovery, report based on how you currently feel. This assessment can be taken online at www.discoverandchange.com/apa

YOUR HISTORY OF INVOLVEMENT

If you have reached a level of sobriety in your recovery, Please answer how you feel now rather than the past.

1. How old were you when you were first introduced to pornography (magazines, Internet pornography, x-rated videos)?

    a.   Between 4 and 8 years old

    b.   Between 9 and 11 years old

    c.   Between 12 and 14 years old

    d.   Between 15 and 18 years old

    e.   Between 19-24 years old

    f.   Older than 25

2. How many times did you see pornographic material before age 18?

    1.   Less than 25

    2.   More than 25 but less than 50

    3.   More than 50 but less than 100

    4.   More than 100 but less than 250

    5.   More than 250 but less than 500

    6.   More than 500 but less than 750

    7.   More than 750

3. How many times would you estimate that you have viewed pornography in your life?

    1.   Less than 100

    2.   More than 100 but less than 250

    3.   More than 250 but less than 500

    4.   More than 500 but less than 750

    5.   More than 750 but less than 1000

    6.   More than 1000 but less than 2500

    7.   More than 2500 times

4. When viewing pornography (magazines, Internet, or videos), how much time will you spend during one episode?

1. 0-15 minutes
2. 15-30 minutes
3. 30 minutes to 1 hour
4. 1-3 hours
5. 3-5 hours
6. 5-6 hours
7. Six or more hours (sometimes all day)

5. In the last year, what is the frequency with which you have viewed pornography?

1. 0 = None
2. 1 = 1-2 times
3. 2 = Every two or three months
4. 3 = Once a month
5. 4 = Every two weeks
6. 5 = Once a week
7. 6 = 3-5 times a week
8. 7 = Almost every day, if not daily

6. What percentage of time each day do you spend thinking or fantasizing about pornography or other sexual behaviors?

1. Less than 5%
2. Between 5%-10%
3. Between 10%-20%
4. Between 20%-30%
5. Between 30%-40%
6. Between 40%-50%
7. Between 50%-60%
8. Between 60%-75%

7. What is the longest period of time that you have gone without pornography in the last year?

   1.   8 months to a year

   2.   6-8 months

   3.   4-6 months

   4.   2-4 months

   5.   1-2 months

   6.   Two weeks to four weeks

   7.   One week

   8.   Three or four days

   9.   One to two days

8. In looking at your involvement in pornography on a scale between 1 and 7, how much influence is pornography having on your life, with one being very little and seven being very significant.

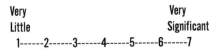

Very Little   **Very Significant**

1------2------3------4------5------6------7

INTENSITY	NEVER	RARELY	SOMETIMES	FREQUENTLY	ALMOST ALWAYS
1. I have experiences where my desire to view pornography is so strong that I will do almost anything to see it.	1	2	3	4	5
2. I find myself taking more and more risks as I view pornography (i.e. viewing in public, while on a bus, or at work).	1	2	3	4	5
3. I have a hard time focusing on tasks because my mind is preoccupied with sexual thoughts, images, or fantasies.	1	2	3	4	5
4. There are times while attending social events, I find myself looking for someone who will act out with me sexually.	1	2	3	4	5
5. Pornography that I used to think was gross or sickening is now common for me to view.	1	2	3	4	5
6. If I don't view pornography when I want to, I become restless.	1	2	3	4	5
7. In addition to pornography, there are other ways I sexually act out.	1	2	3	4	5
8. The sexual thoughts I have about women/men because of my involvement with pornography bother me.	1	2	3	4	5

IMPULSE CONTROL	NEVER	RARELY	SOMETIMES	FREQUENTLY	ALMOST ALWAYS
1. I have told myself many times that I am going to stop looking at pornography only to find myself looking at it again.	1	2	3	4	5
2. I constantly have sexual thoughts that run through my mind.	1	2	3	4	5
3. There are days where all of my free time is spent viewing pornography.	1	2	3	4	5
4. I have viewed pornography three or more times in the same day.	1	2	3	4	5
5. I believe I can stop looking at pornography any time.	5	4	3	2	1

CONSEQUENCES	NEVER	RARELY	SOMETIMES	FREQUENTLY	ALMOST ALWAYS
1. My involvement in pornography has created problems for me in my close relationships (i.e. spouse, parents, girl/boyfriend).	1	2	3	4	5
2. I view pornography knowing it could cost me my job or get me in trouble at school.	1	2	3	4	5
3. Viewing pornography has prevented me from advancing in my career/getting good grades	1	2	3	4	5
4. I hold back in relationships due to my involvement in pornography.	1	2	3	4	5
5. My use of pornography has limited my personal development.	1	2	3	4	5

COPING STRATEGIES	NEVER	RARELY	SOMETIMES	FREQUENTLY	ALMOST ALWAYS
1. When I am stressed I turn to pornography to cope.	1	2	3	4	5
2. Pornography calms my mind when I am feeling overwhelmed.	1	2	3	4	5
3. When I am bored, I view pornography.	1	2	3	4	5
4. When I feel lonely, I turn to pornography.	1	2	3	4	5
5. My mind races so fast that I turn to pornography to calm myself down.	1	2	3	4	5
6. Viewing pornography stresses me out.	0	0	0	0	0

MENTAL HEALTH	NEVER	RARELY	SOMETIMES	FREQUENTLY	ALMOST ALWAYS
1. I feel down and empty due to my involvement with pornography.	1	2	3	4	5
2. I feel like my life is out of control when I view pornography.	1	2	3	4	5
3. My involvement with pornography makes me feel hopeless.	1	2	3	4	5
4. I feel like I am a bad person when I view pornography.	1	2	3	4	5
5. I feel extremely guilty when I view pornography.	1	2	3	4	5
6. I am satisfied with my life.	0	0	0	0	0

	NEVER	RARELY	ONCE A MONTH	TWICE A MONTH	ONCE A WEEK OR MORE
7. I feel good about the things I am doing with my life.	0	0	0	0	0
8. For the most part, I am a happy person.	0	0	0	0	0

SUPPORT IN THE PAST YEAR	NEVER	RARELY	ONCE A MONTH	TWICE A MONTH	ONCE A WEEK OR MORE
1. I attend 12-step groups.	1	2	3	4	5
2. I talk with a sponsor.	1	2	3	4	5
3. I attend therapy.	1	2	3	4	5
4. I talk with a religious leader about my involvement in pornography.	1	2	3	4	5
5. I talk with my family members or friends about my involvement in pornography.	1	2	3	4	5

Have you ever participated in any of the following behaviors?	YES	NO
1. Pay for sex	1	0
2. Watched someone in their home/apartment	1	0
3. Had an affair	1	0
4. Hooked up with someone for a sexual encounter	1	0
5. Visited a topless bar	1	0
6. Touched someone and claimed it was an accident	1	0

Have you ever been diagnosed with any of the following?	YES	NO
1. Anxiety	0	0
2. ADHD	0	0
3. Bipolar disorder	0	0
4. Depression	0	0
5. Narcissism	0	0
6. PTSD	0	0

OTHER PRODUCTS BY DR. KEVIN SKINNER

If you would like to learn more about Relationship Intimacy please visit:
www.discoverandchange.com

If you would like to learn more about Betrayal Trauma please visit:
www.bloomforwomen.com (Use Coupon code: SUNSHINE)

References

CHAPTER 1

1. Buford, Tom (2001). *Your Children & Pornography: A Guide for Parents.* Tommera Press, 2001.

2. Butcher, Andy. "How One Man Unleashed the Porn Plague." *Charisma,* November (2003).

3. Sex on TV: Content and Context. The Kaiser Family Foundation, 5 February, 2001.

4. www.familysafemedia.com, 2003.

5. Internet Filter Review, 2005.

6. Overdosing on Porn, Rebecca Hagelin. www.worldandi.com, March, 2004 and http://www.internetfilterreview.com/internet-pornography-statistics.html.

CHAPTER 2

1. Viscott, David (1996). *Emotional Resilience: Simple Truths for Dealing with the Unfinished Business of Your Past.* Three Rivers Press.

2. Carnes Patrick. (1983). *Out of the Shadows: Understanding Sexual Addiction.* Minneapolis: CompCare Publishers.

3. Pipher, Mary (1997). *The Shelter of Each Other.* Ballantine Books.

4. http://internet-filter-review.toptenreviews.com/internet-pornography-statistics.html.

5. Carnes, Patrick (1991). *Don't Call It Love: Recovery From Sexual Addiction.* Bantam Books.

6. *Sex and Love Addicts Anonymous.* Boston: Augustine Fellowship, Sex and Love Addicts Anonymous, Fellowship Wide Services, 1986. pp. 105.

CHAPTER 3

1. Carnes, Patrick (1991). *Don't Call It Love: Recovery From Sexual Addiction.* Bantam Books.

2. Pert, Candice, cited in Bill Moyers, *Healing and the Mind.* Doubleday, New York, 1993, at 177.

3. Milkman, Harvey B and Sunderwirth, Stanley (1986). *Craving for Ecstasy: The Consciousness and Chemistry of Escape.* Lexington, MA: Lexington Books.

4. *Science,* "New Clues to Brain Dopamine, Control, Cocaine Addiction," February 16, 1996, pp. 983.

CHAPTER 4

1. Peele, Stanton (2004). *7 Tools to Beat Addiction.* Three Rivers Press.

2. Ibid.

CHAPTER 5

1. Prochaska, James O., Norcross, John C., and DiClemente, Carlos C. (1995). *Changing for Good.* New York: Avon Books, 1995.

2. SAMHSA, Office of Applied Studies, National Survey on Drug Use and Health, 2002.

3. Brown, Victor L. (1990). *Human Intimacy.* Bookcraft.

CHAPTER 7

1. Collins, Jim (2001). *Good to Great: Why Some Companies Make the Leap . . . and Others Don't.* Harper Business.

2. Stanley, Thomas (2000). *The Millionaire Mind.* Andrews McMeel Publishing.

CHAPTER 8

1. Peele, Stanton (2004). *7 Tools to Beat Addiction.* Three Rivers Press.

2. Waite, Linda and Gallagher, Maggie (2000). *The Case for Marriage: Why Married People are Happier, Healthier, and Better Off Financially.* Doubleday.

3. Page, Susan (1998). *If I'm So Wonderful Why Am I Still Single?* Three Rivers Press.

4. Carnes, Patrick (1991). *Don't Call It Love: Recovery From Sexual Addiction.* Bantam Books.

CHAPTER 9

1. Peele, Stanton (2004). *7 Tools to Beat Addiction.* Three Rivers Press.

2. McKay, David O. *Teachings of the Presidents of the Church.* Intellectual Reserve (2003).

3. Kincaid, E. Lamar, As quoted in *The Book of Positive Quotations* (1993). Compiled and Arranged by John Cook. Fairview Press.

4. Warren, Neil Clark (2002). *Date . . . Or Soul Mate? How to Know if Someone is Worth Pursuing in Two Dates or Less.* Nelson, Inc.

5. http://www.growthclimate.com

CHAPTER 10

1. Viscott, David (1996). *Emotional Resilience: Simple Truths for Dealing with the Unfinished Business of Your Past.* Three Rivers Press.

2. Taylor, Susan L. (1992). *Lessons in Living.* Anchor Books.

3. Carnes, Patrick (1991). *Don't Call It Love: Recovery From Sexual Addiction.* Bantam Books.

4. McKay, David O. *Teachings of the Presidents of the Church.* Intellectual Reserve (2003).

5. Ibid.

6. Ibid.

My Favorite Books

Carnes, P. (1991). *Don't Call It Love: Recovery From Sexual Addiction.* Bantam Books.

Carnes, P., Delmonico, D., & Griffen, E. (2001). *In the Shadows of the Net: Breaking Free of Compulsive Online Sexual Behavior.* Hazeldon.

Jampolsky, L. (1991). *Healing the Addictive Mind.* Celestial Arts.

Schneider, J. and Weiss, R (2001). *Cybersex Exposed: Simple Fantasy or Obsession?* Hazeldon.

Listen to "Pornography As I See It" with Dr. Kevin Skinner Mondays at 10:00 a.m (EST) on MyExpertSolution Radio Network (www.MyExpertSolution.com). During this show Dr. Skinner answers questions about pornography addiction and interviews top experts around the country.

If you would like to ask Dr. Skinner a question you can do so at www.myexpertsolution.com

Made in the USA
Columbia, SC
24 May 2021